Seal

T0345579

Animal
Series editor: Jonathan Burt

Already published

Albatross Graham Barwell · *Ant* Charlotte Sleigh · *Ape* John Sorenson · *Badger* Daniel Heath Justice
Bear Robert E. Bieder · *Bee* Claire Preston · *Beetle* Adam Dodd · *Beaver* Rachel Poliquin · *Bison*
Desmond Morris · *Camel* Robert Irwin · *Cat* Katharine M. Rogers · *Chicken* Annie Potts · *Cockroach*
Marion Copeland · *Cow* Hannah Velten · *Crocodile* Dan Wylie · *Crow* Boria Sax · *Deer* John Fletcher
Dog Susan McHugh · *Dolphin* Alan Rauch · *Donkey* Jill Bough · *Duck* Victoria de Rijke · *Eagle* Janine
Rogers · *Eel* Richard Schweid · *Elephant* Dan Wylie · *Falcon* Helen Macdonald · *Flamingo* Caitlin R.
Kight · *Fly* Steven Connor · *Fox* Martin Wallen · *Frog* Charlotte Sleigh · *Giraffe* Edgar Williams
Goat Joy Hinson · *Gorilla* Ted Gott and Kathryn Weir · *Guinea Pig* Dorothy Yamamoto
Hare Simon Carnell · *Hedgehog* Hugh Warwick · *Horse* Elaine Walker · *Hyena* Mikita Brottman
Kangaroo John Simons · *Leech* Robert G. W. Kirk and Neil Pemberton · *Leopard* Desmond Morris
Lion Deirdre Jackson · *Lobster* Richard J. King · *Monkey* Desmond Morris · *Moose* Kevin Jackson
Mosquito Richard Jones · *Mouse* Georgie Carroll · *Octopus* Richard Schweid · *Ostrich* Edgar Williams
Otter Daniel Allen · *Owl* Desmond Morris · *Oyster* Rebecca Stott · *Parrot* Paul Carter
Peacock Christine E. Jackson · *Penguin* Stephen Martin · *Pig* Brett Mizelle · *Pigeon* Barbara Allen
Rabbit Victoria Dickenson · *Rat* Jonathan Burt · *Rhinoceros* Kelly Enright · *Salmon* Peter Coates
Seal Victoria Dickenson · *Shark* Dean Crawford · *Skunk* Alyce Miller · *Snail* Peter Williams
Snake Drake Stutesman · *Sparrow* Kim Todd · *Spider* Katarzyna and Sergiusz Michalski
Swallow Angela Turner · *Swan* Peter Young · *Tiger* Susie Green · *Tortoise* Peter Young
Trout James Owen · *Vulture* Thom van Dooren · *Walrus* John Miller and Louise Miller
Whale Joe Roman · *Wolf* Garry Marvin

Seal

Victoria Dickenson

REAKTION BOOKS

This book is dedicated to the people of the sea
and those who follow them into their secret ways

Published by
REAKTION BOOKS LTD
Unit 32, Waterside
44–48 Wharf Road
London N1 7UX, UK
www.reaktionbooks.co.uk

First published 2016
Copyright © Victoria Dickenson 2016

Printed and bound in China by C&C Offset Printing Co. Ltd

A catalogue record for this book is available from the British Library

ISBN 9 781 78023 489 2

Contents

Introduction

The sea had been choppy and the ferry heaved and rolled on the short run from the small island of St Pierre to the almost-mainland of Newfoundland, a vast dark rock in the waters. By the time we began the drive on the single road leading north along the Burin Peninsula, the sky had cleared, and the hurricane had blown itself out. We stopped at a long, sandy beach as small waves rolled in and the sinking sun shot gilt from beneath a dark line of cloud. We sat on barely dry rock and looked out to sea, and there she was, a dark head in the glowing water. We watched and she watched, occasionally slipping under the surface and then re-emerging a short distance further along the shore. Our mutual regard lasted until we stood up, and she vanished, one moment there, the next only the grey sea.

I did not grow up along the coasts of the North Atlantic, meaning that until we moved to Newfoundland my acquaintance with seals in their natural habitat was non-existent. Seals were characters in children's books, like Sammy the Seal, or perched on drums in vintage circus posters. This first seal was a revelation. I knew instantly that it was a seal – a dark head in the water, what else could it be? But I was unprepared for the long, steady gaze that watched me as I watched her.

I have seen many seals since that first encounter, but always there is the sense that I am as much observed as observing. The

Dark head in the water, a harbour seal.

seal's gaze is distinctive – it is not the unfathomable, measuring glare of the lion or bear, or the furtive glance of the rabbit. Seals gaze upon humans as neither predator nor prey. We, on the other hand, have for millennia preyed on seals, and while it is not surprising that they keep a weather eye on the two-legged ones on shore, their steady regard belies fear. The seal's gaze seems curious, and, above all, familiar. People who make their living from the sea and live most closely with the wild seals accuse them not only of bad behaviour – stealing the catch, ripping nets and destroying fish traps – but of knowingly taunting them, waving a lazy flipper as they disappear below the waves. An infuriated sixteenth-century monk complained that when he chased the seal from his lines, 'Cares he not nor listens,/ But begins to grin/ And wink his eyes', and worse, slaps the water, dives and releases a noxious, flatulent cloud.[1]

The seals may compete for our catches, but they often also appear to long for our company, and there are many stories of seals following boats, listening to the music of flute or pipe, even forsaking their own kind to live comfortably with human companions. William Dunbar, a nineteenth-century British naturalist, cast an almost Darwinian eye on this behaviour. While bathing with his pupils in the aptly named Seal Bay in the Outer Hebrides, he remarked how

> numbers of these creatures invariably made their appearance, especially if the weather was calm and sunny, and the sea smooth, crowding around us at the distance of a few yards, and looking as if they had some kind of notion that we were of the same species, or at least genus, with themselves.[2]

It is hard to imagine a creature more distant from the human species in bodily form, habits and habitat than the seal, yet our mutual regard tells of a long, shared history of interaction, and perhaps of something more. Seals, like dogs, are said to understand human language, and unlike the mute rabbit or the growling bear, they call and murmur to each other in a language we think we just might grasp, so familiar are the tones.[3] They also weep and wail, grin and wave, and look us in the eye – demanding what? Kinship? Those who have studied seals and their history describe them as unique, uncanny, aberrant – evoking complex reactions in researchers, naturalists, those who fish and those with whom they share the shores.

There are, of course, many animals who feature largely in the human imagination. They are the characters in beast stories, fables and fairy tales. Among them are clever Mr Fox and Br'er Rabbit, Puss in Boots and the bad mouse Hunca Munca; there are seven

Seal cove,
Newfoundland.

swan brothers and a frog prince, the Monkey King and three little pigs, the big bad wolf and the treacherous snake of Eden. All their stories are stories about us. Dressed in boots and coats, carrying swords and whispering in our ears, the animals act out our tales, embody our best and worst traits, and serve to make us regard our own behaviour and assumptions with a critical eye. There are almost no such stories about seals. They do not feature in bestiaries, and there are no fables about greedy seals and bunches of grapes. They do not dress in borrowed finery, nor do they behave like flippered humans. They behave like seals, and even when they assume our form, as in tales they sometimes do, they are not us. They remain seals. Books about seals may begin as wild animal studies, but will end somewhere in the queer, uncomfortable place where distinctions between human observer and animal subject waver and cloud, and the lens becomes a mirror, the enquiring gaze returned.

Seals, with some exceptions, live at the ends of the earth, and to watch seals in the places they inhabit by choice is the privilege of few. In the transoceanic barrens of southern Newfoundland, you can take a path along a breathtakingly beautiful stream that gallops and frets down the hills to end in a shallow cove. There is a small crescent of sandy beach, and the cove is dotted with large flat rocks. A rocky islet – home to black-backed and herring gulls – shelters the cove from the surging Atlantic waters. It is here that one clan comes to take the air, to lie content on sun-warmed rocks, with an occasional dip into kelpy waters. To see the seals in repose, you must lower yourself down onto your knees on the hillside and crawl along the ridge, finally wriggling along on your belly through the crowberry and mossy rocks until you can just peer over the edge. If you are quiet, and if you do not show your head above the hill line, you can watch the rotund adults loll on the rocks, flippers waving, or the lithe juveniles slide into the water and chase about in the kelp. The water is a clear, pale green and from this height you can see how fast and powerfully they move under the surface, in contrast to the great to-do required to haul themselves out on to a rock. One quick movement from the

Grey seals.

hilltop, however, and those on the rocks explode into the water, and disappear. As you walk away, looking back, you see that some return, their heads emerging one by one above the still surface of the cove, watching you watching them.

These are wary harbour seals. In contrast, the great grey seals that claim the waters around nearby Cape Race (where the signal from the sinking *Titanic* was first received) are seemingly oblivious to watchers on the cliff tops. Perhaps it is that their wave-washed rocks are so inaccessible, or that their vast bulk makes them less timid. The huge males snort and neigh, but occasionally a young seal, a female, slips away from the group and bullets through the transparent water, rounds the point, and looks up, perhaps pensively, at our black heads silhouetted against that other ocean of air.

These seals belong to an ancient order of mammals; they have shared the coasts and islands with our species for as long as we have inhabited them. Our encounters with them have varied from peaceful co-existence to all-out war, and our relationship with them is key in the ongoing debate over how we live together on our terraqueous globe. As they have always done, the seals are watching us.

1 True Seals

You do not have to be a biologist to tell a seal from any other mammal. Everybody knows what a seal looks like – streamlined body, rounded head, large dark eyes, long whiskers, small tail, flippers. The group comprising seals, sea lions, fur seals and walruses is so distinctive that biologists have classified them as members of a single order, the Pinnipedia, characterized by zoologist Victor Scheffer as 'isolated, aberrant, unique'.[1] 'Pinniped' means 'wing-footed', an apt description of their hind limbs that, like divers' fins, give them wings in the water. Pinnipeds are grouped with the marine mammals, a broad spectrum of warmblooded animals that have adapted to life in the sea, and which includes the cetaceans (whales, porpoises and dolphins), as well as manatees, sea otters and polar bears. In terms of adaptation, pinnipeds inhabit the middle of that spectrum, neither wholly aquatic like the whales, nor decidedly terrestrial like bears, but as Scheffer described them – 'queer amphibious animals living at the interface of land and sea'.[2] There is, in fact, continuing debate among biologists as to whether seals are more closely related to ancient bears or to otters, but recent discoveries in the Canadian Arctic have shed more light on the seals' ambiguous history.

Archetypal pinniped, a juvenile harp seal.

WALKING SEAL

In 2007 an all-terrain vehicle carrying researchers from the Canadian Museum of Nature in Ottawa ran out of fuel and became stuck in the mud on Devon Island, far north of the Arctic Circle. Two of the field team offered to walk back to camp for a tank of fuel, while a field assistant and a senior palaeontologist remained with the vehicle. Taking advantage of the opportunity, the two left behind began to poke about for possible finds in the surrounding rocky outcrop. In frustration, the young field assistant kicked the ground with the toe of her boot, turning over a dark object she recognized at once as a piece of bone. By the time the other members of the team had returned, the two scientists were excitedly digging deep into the dirt, unearthing a major find. Over the next two days, the team screened 250 kg (551 lb) of pebbly matrix, beginning what became a several-year-long

14

process of excavating the nearly complete skeleton of an animal they quickly realized represented something quite new, and a 'missing link' in the story of pinniped evolution.

Fossil seals are not new to science; more than 50 extinct seals have been identified. In the Miocene epoch, some 25 to 18 million years ago, individuals of the genus *Enaliarctos*, considered an ancestor of modern pinnipeds, swam off the coast of what is now Oregon in the U.S. and looked not unlike the modern seal, with webbed feet, a short tail, large eyes and long whiskers. But what kind of animal preceded the ancestral seal? How did a small carnivore go from stalking on land to swimming through prehistoric seas? Over the past decades, researchers have unearthed other fossilized remains of very early 'walking seals', but the near-completeness and good state of preservation of the Devon Island skeleton enabled Dr Natalia Rybczynski and her team to reconstruct not only the animal's appearance but its mode of life, illustrating the adaptations required to live 'at the intersection of land and sea'.[3] The fossil had a skull like a seal, and a body like a muscular otter. Dr Rybczynski named him (the team unearthed the baculum, or penis bone) *Puijila darwini*. *Puijila* is the Inuktitut word for a young seal, and *darwini* refers of course to

Nobumichi Tamura, illustration of the fossil seal *Puijila darwinii*.

15

Charles Darwin, who almost 150 years earlier in *On the Origin of Species* had speculated how a land animal might be transformed into one at home in the water:

> A strictly terrestrial animal, by occasionally hunting for food in shallow water, then in streams or lakes, might at last be converted into an animal so thoroughly aquatic as to brave the open ocean.[4]

Puijila had braved not the open ocean but a freshwater lake that had formed in an impact crater on Devon Island. He swam with both front and hind flippers, and shared the marshy waters and shoreline with a proto-swan, varieties of fish, rabbits, rodents and ducks (bones of the last two were found fossilized in his stomach).[5] The discovery of *Puijila* supports Darwin's insight that the evolution of pinnipeds included a freshwater transitional phase, but also supports the hypothesis that the Arctic, where the seal is today such a prominent member of the native fauna, was an early centre of pinniped evolution, with different groups dispersing southwards over time.

Puijila's use of both fore and hind limbs to paddle through the water points to another important hypothesis about the origin of seals. Despite the similarities in their overall appearance and habits, there had been speculation among scientists that fur seals, sea lions and walruses, who propel themselves with their fore flippers, shared one common ancestor, and all the other seals, who swim with their hind flippers, another. Increasingly, however, the pinnipeds are considered by scientists to have a monophyletic origin; that is, all the varied members of the family, from long-tusked walruses and giant elephant seals, to the familiar harbour seal and the performing sea lions, descended from a common ancestor who may have closely resembled *Puijila*.

Friedrich Justin Bertuch, *Amphibien*, I, from *Bilderbuch für Kinder* (A Picture Book for Children, 1800).

Today, the pinnipeds are represented by two distinct lineages that scientists believe diverged over 33 million years ago – the superfamilies Otarioidea and Phocoidea. The Otarioidea are composed of two families, the Otariidae and Odobenidae, the first consisting of five genera of sea lion and two of fur seals, and the second comprising only one living member, the walrus. The Phocidae family, referred to as 'true seals', comprise eighteen different species divided into two main subfamilies, the Monachinae

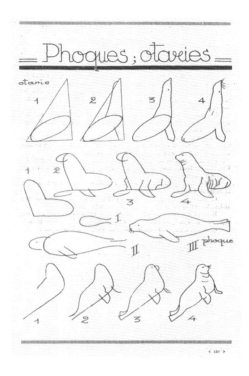

Distinguishing a phocid from an otariid. Illustration from R. and L. Lambry, *Les animaux tels qu'ils sont* (1949).

and the Phocinae. Both Otarioidea and the Phocidae share many of the characteristics that over millennia fitted them to their queer amphibious life. They gave up agility on land, but gained immense ability to move swiftly and effortlessly through a new, denser medium. They can stay at sea for sometimes months at a time, and can dive to remarkable depths. They tolerate the cold of polar waters and ocean depths, and see almost equally well on land as underwater. They can also hear remarkably well underwater and in many cases nearly as acutely on land. Their sensitive whiskers (vibrissae) help them navigate cloudy waters, and in the case of the lumbering walrus who sports a generous 'moustache'

Pinnipeds, from the *Brockhaus and Efron Encyclopedic Dictionary* (1890–1907).

18

1 Обыкновенный тюлень (Phoca vitulina). Длина 1—0,90 м

2. Морской левъ (Otaria jubata). Длина 2—3 м.

3. Моржъ (Trichechus rosmarus). Длина 4—5 м.

Kiotari, a Pacific harbour seal, with big eyes and a prominent moustache, rescued by the Marine Mammal Center, California.

of 600 to 700 whiskers (more than other seals and most land carnivores), also help locate their prey – molluscs on the muddy sea floor.

These two great groupings differ, however, in significant ways. For those not fortunate enough to live along the seal-thronged coasts of the Atlantic or the Pacific, the image of the

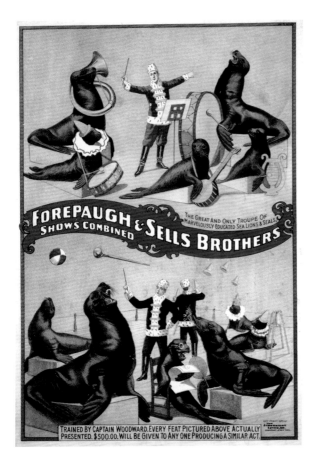

An advertisement for a Forepaugh & Sells Brothers show, which included 'The Great and Only Troupe of Marvelously Educated Sea Lions & Seals', c. 1899.

seal is likely to be a circus seal, flippers splayed, perched on a drum with a ball balanced on a bewhiskered nose. But the circus performer is usually a California sea lion, and his posture on the drum reveals an important difference between the two branches of pinnipeds. Nineteenth-century scientists classified the pinnipeds as either 'walkers' or 'wrigglers'.[6] Fur seals, sea lions and, to

A harbour (common) seal on the Isle of Skye.

a lesser extent, walruses can fold their hind flippers under them, raise their upper bodies, and 'walk' on land. Sea lions in particular are so agile out of water that they can climb stairs, and swing along city streets.[7] The phocids are the wrigglers. Pulling themselves along with their fore flippers, hind flippers dragging behind, these rotund seals bounce, hump and lurch their way along, their smooth bodies better suited to sliding over ice in the cold oceans where many live than moving over rough ground. In the water, sea lions and fur seals 'fly' through the sea, using their long fore flippers like wings. Phocid seals propel themselves by moving their hind flippers in a kind of sculling motion. Walruses, like the ur-seal *Puijila*, tend to use both flippers, sculling with the hind and manoeuvring with the fore.

The otariids – fur seals and sea lions – are also distinguished by their possession of pinnae, or outer ears. The walrus and the phocids have none, and the 'true' seals are thus commonly known as the 'earless' seals. Aristotle suggested that the absence of ears was an aberration in a quadruped, the result of deformity, but it is rather an adaptation to the life aquatic, as is their smooth rounded shape.[8] This book is about the sleek, earless seals, so at home in the waters of the world, and so varied in their habits, habitats and appearance.

The phocids are the embodiment of *phoke*, the Greek word for seal, in turn derived from the Sanskrit for a 'swollen or plump animal'.[9] They are indeed rotund creatures. Peter Simon Pallas, the German naturalist who explored eastern Russia from 1768 to 1774, was amazed by the small and evidently very plump Caspian seal (*Pusa caspica*):

> The Seal of the Caspian is much fatter in autumn than those of the Baltic which I have seen. They appear more like a skin filled with oil than an animal, as you can scarcely recognise their head and fore paws for the fat.[10]

The 'fat' that Pallas refers to is the blubber layer found under the skin, which in some seasons can account for up to 50 per cent of the body weight of the seal.[11] While all phocids are well blubbered, they differ considerably in size, but are on average larger than land-based carnivores. A weasel, for example, may weigh only 25 g (0.9 oz), and the Arctic fox on average about 3.5 kg (7.7 lb), but the ringed seal, one of the most common and smallest of the Arctic seals, weighs in at 50 kg (110 lb). There are in fact no small marine mammals, and buoyed by their dense watery habitat, seals can grow surprisingly large. The Caspian seal is one of the smallest of its kind, at around 86 kg (190 lb); the widespread harbour seal (*Phoca vitulina*) weighs between 85 and 135 kg (187 and 298 lb), while the Antarctic leopard seal (*Hydrurga leptonyx*) goes from 200 to 600 kg, and the gargantuan male southern elephant seal (*Mirounga leonina*) manoeuvres a bulk of

Weighing a spotted seal (*Phoca largha*), Alaska, 1978.

Scientist holding a ribbon seal pup, Alaska, June 1978.

Leopard seal, lying on the ice.

A male southern elephant seal.

up to 4,000 kg (8,818 lb), about half the size of his terrestrial namesake, the African elephant, but still a marine giant. Elephant seals (*Mirounga* spp.) and grey seals (*Halichoerus grypus*) also display a pronounced sexual dimorphism, or difference in size between male and female, which in the case of the southern elephant seal might mean that the male outweighs the relatively petite female of 400 kg (882 lb) by a factor of ten to one.

True seals swim all the oceans of the world, and some of its fresh waters. The two phocid subfamilies – the phocines and monachines – differ primarily in their choice of habitat. The phocines cling to the ancestral home in the northern hemisphere, but the monachines have spread southwards to temperate and tropical waters, and to the Antarctic seas. There are more phocid species in the Arctic, but greater absolute numbers of seals in the

24

Crabeater seals.

Antarctic, particularly of the monachine crabeater seal (*Lobodon carcinophagus*), which accounts for the fact that phocids today make up roughly 90 per cent of the world's pinniped population.[12]

THE MONACHINES: SEALS OF THE SOUTH

The monachines include three distinct groups: *Monachus* (the monk seals), *Mirounga* (the elephant seals) and Lobodontini (four genera of Antarctic seals). In contrast to the swarms of crabeater seals, the remaining small populations of monk seals are critically endangered. The Mediterranean monk seal (*Monachus monachus*),[13] hailed by Homer in *The Odyssey* as 'the brood of the lovely child of Ocean', has been hunted for millennia for skins and oil, or killed as a competitor to human fishers. This ancient seal now breeds reluctantly in the wine-dark seas of the Aegean or along the shores of the Mediterranean, and is considered a 'bottleneck population' by scientists, so reduced in numbers that it no longer has the genetic variability nor resilience to repopulate ancestral waters. This problem is exacerbated by disease, loss of habitat and continued predation by humans.

First classified as 'endangered' in 1966, almost two-thirds of the seal population on the aptly named Côte des Phoques ('Seal Coast') in the Western Sahara were decimated in a sudden die-off in 1996 (perhaps caused by toxic algae), making the Mediterranean monk seal the most critically endangered marine mammal in the world. According to the International Union for Conservation of Nature (IUCN), only about 350–450 seals remain in the wild, in tiny remnant colonies along the shores of the sea they once filled.[14] A similar fate probably accounted for the extinction in modern times of another of the monachines, the Caribbean monk seal (*Neomonachus tropicalis*), first recorded by Christopher Columbus in 1494. In 1846 the English naturalist Philip Henry Gosse de - scribed what must have been by then the members of a declining population: 'They seemed to delight in basking in the sun, and to huddle together, and grunt out their pleasure in each others'

A monk seal on a rock by the shore. Coloured etching by W. H. Lizars after James Stewart, from Sir William Jardine, *The Naturalist's Library*, vol. XXIV (1839).

company.' The seals were deemed 'very easily killed or captured alive', and yielded a great deal of oil. They also provided a kind of sport:

> One of my informants says that as he was sailing about the islands fishing and wrecking, he and his party discovered a number of Seals on one of them, and went on shore to kill some, merely 'for fun'.[15]

Last seen in 1952, these seals of the Caribbean islands were officially declared extinct in 2008.

Monk seals appear not to have been fortunate in their choices of habitat. The Hawaiian monk seal (*Neomonachus schauinslandi*) also inhabits some of the most beautiful tropical islands, competing with human species for sandy beaches and aquamarine waters. This seal is considered the most primitive of the phocids, a 'living fossil', which arrived in the Hawaiian islands millions of years ago, long before the first Polynesians. Now also declared critically endangered, scientists recorded just over 1,200 individuals in 2014.[16] The Hawaiian population is so small, and the competition for the few breeding females so great, that during the mating season in some colonies female seals have been killed by group mobbing, further reducing the viability of the species. Contrast this handful of individuals with the abundance of their cousins, the crabeaters, whose icy Antarctic shores pose little temptation for sunbathers or surfers.

Another monachine species, the northern elephant seal (*Mirounga angustirostris*), has also experienced an extreme genetic bottleneck. Inhabiting the coastal waters of California and Mexico, the northern elephants were almost exterminated by hunting in the early nineteenth century. By the mid-1880s it has been estimated that no more than twenty seals may have survived the slaughter.[17] Even as late as 1892, when eight seals were discovered on Guadalupe Island, seven were killed by museum collectors. Fortunately, for an animal once referred to as 'one of the bygone wonders of the animal kingdom',[18] the population has made a

Hawaiian monk seal in the waters off Laysan Island, Hawaii, June 1969.

dramatic recovery, growing from a handful to over 175,000 individuals, the seals even recolonizing abandoned habitats. Despite this success, northern elephant seals exhibit dramatically reduced genetic variability when compared to other mammals and to their own southern congeners. (The northern population is specifically distinct from the southern.) Scientists fear that this lack of genetic diversity will endanger the nascent populations, making them more susceptible to disease or environmental disruption, and bringing these northern seals once again into the shadow zone of an endangered species.

Like the monk seals, the northern elephant seals were unfortunate in their choice of habitat, breeding on islands off the coasts of California and Mexico, where they came to the attention of the nineteenth-century blubber hunters. Southern elephant seals, despite their relative isolation, also suffered greatly from

Elephant seals on the beach at Piedras Blancas, California.

the depredations of the hunt. They were first described in the account of the circumnavigation of the globe by George Anson, whose crew encountered the gigantic beasts on the Juan Fernandez Islands off the coast of Chile in 1741. Anson brought back to London the first skull of the southern species, and reported of their prodigious bulk and the quantity of oil that could be derived from it, which began the process that led to their near-extinction:

it is so extraordinary an animal, I conceive it well merits a particular description. They are in size when arrived at their full growth, from twelve to twenty feet in length, and from eight to fifteen in circumference. They are extremely fat, so that, after having cut through the skin, which is about an inch in thickness, there is at least a foot of fat before you can come at either lean or bones; and we experienced more than once, that the fat of some of the largest afforded us a butt of oil.[19]

They were at first called 'Sea-Lyons', but quickly became known as the elephants of the seas. A specimen at the Liverpool Museum, known as 'The Great Seal', was drawn by William Lizars, the engraver, who described it as 'a wonderful monster . . . compared with any ordinary Seal three or four feet long, it appears exactly like an Elephant when compared to a sheep'.[20] Antoine Joseph Pernetty, an eighteenth-century French naturalist, was equally amazed by these 'monsters' during his sojourn in the Falkland Islands:

At first I had no adequate conception of their prodigious size. When at the distance of about a thousand yards they looked like little mountains, and it was only on coming close that I formed a correct idea of them.[21]

'Sea lion and lioness', male and female elephant seals during the mating season. Coloured etching, after engraving in *Atlas to Anson's Voyage round the World* (1745).

The 'little mountains' were likely the males, which can be many times the size of the females. The males are of course distinguished not only by their girth, but by their long, pendulous noses, which also account for their common name. The northern elephant seals sport a lengthier snout than those of the southern, so long in fact that it sometimes gets caught in their teeth.[22] These seals also exhibit one of the most extreme cases of polygyny among mammals. During the two months of the spring breeding season, 'beachmasters' spar for control of a harem, which in the case of an alpha male may number up to 150 females. Anson's sailors styled these successful bulls the 'bashaws', who 'generally lay surrounded with a seraglio of females'.[23]

During the few months of breeding and moult that they spend on land, the seals clump together on stony beaches, but the rest of the year they are at sea, covering vast distances. Not only are they among the farthest-ranging migrants of the animal world, but they are among the deepest divers. Elephant seals make 'vertical commutes' to pursue prey (chiefly squid) several times a day, diving to depths of 400–800 m (1,312–2,625 ft) for 20 to 30 minutes at a time. A northern elephant seal has, however, been recorded reaching twice that depth (1,599 m or 5,246 ft), and a female has remained underwater for nearly two hours, almost matching the sperm whale (the deepest diving of all mammals) in submarine endurance.

Lobodontine seals favour the icy Southern Ocean, and this isolated habitat has helped somewhat to preserve their populations from human predation. Crabeater, leopard, Ross (*Ommatophoca rossii*) and Weddell (*Leptonychotes weddellii*) seals are ice-lovers, or pagophiles. The first three inhabit the pack ice, or floating ice, which forms on the surface of the sea in the Antarctic winter. By September, that ice will cover an area twice the size of the continental United States in a layer about a metre thick. The ice moves with wind and currents, and here the seals haul out to breed, moult and rest. The movement of the ice causes a unique geography of hillocks, ridges, crevices and leads that provide shelter, protection and access to food sources in the waters below. Weddell seals are the most southerly ranging mammal in the world (except for the human species), and surprisingly spend much of their year below the fast ice – the ice sheets that are shore-fast, or attached

Two 'beachmasters' (bull northern elephant seals), Piedras Blancas, California.

to the land. They use their teeth to gnaw breathing holes in these thick sheets, and remain below the surface, resting on interior ice shelves; they can be heard calling beneath the ice all winter.[24] Weddell and leopard seals will also haul out on land when ice is unavailable, and Weddell seals breed on South Georgia Island where there is no ice. The lobodontines, whose name means 'lobed-tooth', also remind us that all seals are carnivores, even if some of their food is very tiny. Antarctic krill (*Euphausia superba*) forms 94 to 98 per cent of the food of the crabeater seal. As a result of their exclusive diet, the crabeaters possess some of the most strongly modified teeth of any mammal, their cheek teeth having evolved to resemble a dental portcullis. The seal gulps mouthfuls of krill, then closes its jaws and strains the water through the small openings in its teeth.[25] The biomass of krill in the Southern

Seals on ice in Antarctica, 2013.

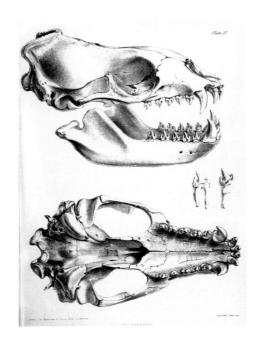

Leopard seal skull, showing specialized teeth, illustration from Benjamin Waterhouse Hawkins, *The Zoology of the Voyage of the HMS 'Erebus' and 'Terror', under the command of Captain Sir James Clark Ross, during the years 1839 to 1843* (1844).

Ocean is estimated at over 500,000,000 tons, or twice that of the human biomass in the world, which is just as well, since crabeaters are among the most numerous large mammals on earth. The abundance of crabeaters is welcomed by leopard seals, who not only slurp up krill but enjoy the flesh of their congeners. It is reported that almost all crabeaters over the age of one year bear the characteristic parallel tooth scars from encounters with their voracious cousins. Leopard seals are also fond of penguins, and one scientist observed a very successful and evidently hungry seal consume six Adélie penguins in 70 minutes.[26] The leopard seal is aptly named, and its ferocity and determination when stalking prey are legendary, even if the prey is supposedly top of the food chain.

A leopard seal
showing teeth.

Thomas Orde-Lees was a member of Sir Ernest Shackleton's
Antarctic expedition when he encountered the leopard of the ice:

> Returning from a hunting trip, Orde-Lees, traveling on skis
> across the rotting surface of the ice, had just about reached
> camp when an evil, knob-like head burst out of the water
> just in front of him . . . The animal – a sea leopard – sprang
> out of the water and came after him, bounding across the
> ice with the peculiar rocking-horse gait of a seal on land.
> The beast looked like a small dinosaur, with a long, serpen-
> tine neck. After a half-dozen leaps, the sea leopard had
> almost caught up with Orde-Lees when it unaccountably
> wheeled and plunged again into the water . . . he was about
> to cross to safe ice when the sea leopard's head exploded
> directly in front of him. The animal had tracked his shadow
> across the ice. It made a savage lunge for Orde-Lees with its
> mouth open, revealing an enormous array of saw-like teeth.
> Orde-Lees' shouts for help turned to screams . . .[27]

Orde-Lees survived his encounter when his companion shot the animal. No doubt the penguins were not so lucky.[28]

THE PHOCINES: SEALS OF THE NORTH

According to the Inuit, the northern phocine seals are the children of a sea goddess. Sedna is the powerful spirit of the Arctic seas, and when her fingers were cut off by her father (it is a long story to be told later, in chapter Three), they were transformed into seals and walruses. No tropical beaches beckon the phocines, and the majority inhabit the circumpolar waters of the Arctic. Like the seals of the Southern Ocean, they are, with few exceptions, pagophilic, birthing their young on the rafting floes of the pack ice, or on shore-fast ice sheets. Their common names reflect distinguishing characteristics of their appearance, easily seen against the Arctic white: the harp seal (*Phoca groenlandica*) has a harp-shaped 'saddle-back'; the ribbon seal (*Histriophoca fasciata*) a white band; the bearded seal (*Erignathus barbatus*) a charming walrus-like moustache; the ringed seal (*Pusa hispida*) a fur coat spotted with grey rings; and the hooded seal (*Cystophora cristata*), perhaps strangest of all, an inflatable 'crest'. While elephant seals may sport long noses, the male hooded seal has an unusually flexible nasal cavity that in mature animals forms a kind of bulbous appendage on the front of the head. When the seal is excited, the sac can be inflated to about the size of two footballs. Even more surprisingly, the male has an unusual ability to blow out his own nose. When displaying to attract the female of the species, the male hooded seal inflates the nasal membrane of the left nostril into a pink balloon, which he waves about in a presumably sexually appealing manner.

Some phocines are found only in the western hemisphere (hooded, harp and grey), while others swim the North Pacific to the Sea of Japan (ribbon and largha or *Phoca largha*). The ringed seal is truly circumpolar, but two related species have very restricted distributions. The Caspian seal, whose blubbery bulk so impressed Pallas, exclusively inhabits the brackish waters of the Caspian Sea, which became landlocked 5 million years ago. This population is now endangered from a host of factors – disease, pollution, predators both human and animal, competition from commercial fishing, disturbance from shipping associated with oilfield developments, and climate change, as the ice fields on which the seals breed slowly shrink.[29]

Henry W. Elliot, illustration of harp seals from specimens in the u.s. National Museum.

A hooded, or crested, seal. Coloured etching by W. H. Lizars after James Stewart, from Sir William Jardine, *The Naturalist's Library*, vol. xxiv (1839).

THE CRESTED SEAL

An adult male ribbon seal, Ozernoy Gulf, Russia.

The Baikal seal, or nerpa (*Pusa sibirica*), has an equally distinctive habitat, living in one of the world's largest freshwater lakes, and unlike the Caspian, its population is relatively stable.[30] The Baikal are among the smallest of seals, and also may be the longest lived. Females continue to produce pups into their mid-forties, and there are records of adult males and females surviving into their fifties.[31] While many seals live fifteen to 30 years or more, this longevity for both male and female is surprising. Among many seal species, males appear to die young, succumbing to the stresses of fighting, breeding and defending territory. Very few northern elephant seal males, for example, who fight to acquire and maintain 'harems', survive the eight or nine years necessary to achieve breeding age.[32]

The harbour seal (*Phoca vitulina*) has the widest distribution of any phocid, and is found throughout the coastal waters of the northern hemisphere as far south as Baja California in the Pacific and Portugal in the Atlantic. The lives of harbour seals and people have intersected for millennia, and as far as scientific classification is concerned, they represent the archetypal seal. In *Systema Naturae*, published in 1758, the great taxonomist Carl Linnaeus

Freshwater seals (nerpas) on Lake Baikal.

named four members of the tribe of *Phoca* – one sea lion, one elephant seal, one walrus and *Phoca vitulina*, the 'sea calf'. Linnaeus described the pinnipeds as 'a dirty, curious, quarrelsome tribe, easily tamed, and polygamous; flesh tender and succulent; fat and skin useful', a description that might well have been based on personal observation of these seals along the Swedish coasts.[33]

Harbour seals were well known long before Linnaeus gave them a scientific name, and their common name reflects their preferred habitat. Robin's Reef (now Robbins Reef) in New York Harbor was named after the seals (*robyn* in Dutch) that once hauled out there. They have also been known to frequent fresh water, and in North America have been recorded in the St Lawrence River as far up as Montreal, in Lake Champlain in Vermont, as well as 200 km (124 miles) up the Columbia River on a tributary known as the 'dog river', named perhaps for the 'sea dogs' who were seen in its waters. In northern Quebec, the Ungava seal, a subspecies of harbour seal (*Phoca vitulina mellonae*), swims and breeds in the appropriately named Upper and Lower Seal Lakes (*Lacs des Loups Marins*). Here, 240 m (787 ft) above sea level and 250 km (155 miles) from Hudson Bay, there remains an isolated relict tribe of perhaps 600 seals, which several thousand years ago followed the fish to these inland lakes.[34] Harbour seals, while they frequent cold waters, are not, however, ice-lovers. They haul out on land to give birth, and since their range brings them close to human settlement, they have adapted to the possibility of disturbance. Their pups can swim at first tide, and mother and pup nurse in the shallow waters. The pup's white coat, or lanugo, is evidence that they were once ice-breeders. While the lanugo is a marvellous insulator for a pup resting on ice, it is ineffective when wet;

'Seals', an 18th-century engraving by Peter Mazell.

harbour seal pups are, instead, born with a dark warm coat, and their downy lanugo is moulted prior to birth, as a nineteenth-century observer noted:

> the native young seal sheds its fur in the whelping bag, for after it is whelped a lump of white fur, about the size of a large goose egg, nicely packed and perfectly dry, covered with a viscous matter, is seen floating about in the water, it looks like a little mass of froth.[35]

The grey seals, among the largest of the phocines, also breed primarily on land, and the white coats of their offspring at birth also suggest a more recent association with ice, though they now loll on sandy beaches or grassy islands. The Gulf of St Lawrence herd still breeds on the fast ice along the river, as do some of the less common Baltic population, but most have traditional haul-ing-out places on rocky coasts, sandbars and islands. Grey seals,

'Antur 1', a Kuril seal (*Phoca vitulina stejnegeri*), a subspecies of the harbour seal.

Grey seal with the species' distinctive nose.

or 'sea pigs', are easily distinguished by their large size, and the long, arched noses of the males – some call it a 'Roman' nose; in Canada they are known as 'horseheads'. The majority of the global population lives around the British Isles, where they are woven deeply into the life of the human inhabitants of remote and rocky shores. These are the 'selkies', and their stories are told in chapter Three.

STRANGE HABITS

While we know a great deal about seals on land, we know less about their adaptations to life at sea. Given their habits, distribution and variety, they are, as scientists have pointed out, charismatic but difficult to study. What has been evident to observers since classical times is that seals are vocal animals. They talk and sing, both above and below the water, and have been named as much for their vocalizations as their appearance:

> Seals utter a variety of cries, from which they have derived such various names as Sea-dogs, Sea-calves, Sea-wolves, etc. Some have a barking note, others a kind of tender bleat, or a cry more or less resembling that of a child. The cry of the young is usually more or less pathetic, while that of the adults is heavier and hoarser.[36]

Elephant seals, which live in dense congregations of females, pups and bellowing beachmasters, are particularly vocal, as George Anson and his sailors observed:

> The cry of the female and the young male resembles the lowing of an ox; but, in the adult males, the proboscis gives such an inflexion to their voice, that it is something like that kind of noise which may be produced by gurgling. This hoarse and singular cry is heard at a great distance, and is wild and frightful; and in these dreary regions during the stormy nights which sometimes occur, on being suddenly roused from slumber by the confused bellowings of these colossal animals, congregated near your bivouac, you can scarcely resist being seized with a momentary panic.[37]

Like the elephants, grey seals also haul out in dense packs, and sing to each other. The song of grey seals, at least in the Western Atlantic, comprises seven different calls. They wail, moan, warble, cry, cough, snort, roar, and on Sable Island off Nova Scotia, they also yodel. Underwater, they click, knock, 'trrot', 'rup' and roar. The solitary bearded seal is also known to sing a complex series of trills underwater, lasting more than a minute, and these can be heard at a distance of 25 km (15.5 miles).[38] The Weddell seals are especially vocal underwater, where they whistle, chirp, trill and buzz. Their calls can also be heard through the ice, allowing swimming seals to communicate with their companions on the surface. During the breeding season, the males use a repertoire of particular sounds in displays to maintain their submarine territories. Harbour seals on land typically belch, grunt and snort, but apparently with a little encouragement can develop a wider vocabulary. When 'Hoover', an orphaned seal raised by human caregivers in Maine in the U.S., was seven years old and a resident of the New England Aquarium, he began to 'talk', imitating human speech with a Boston accent. He could say his name and phrases like 'Hello there', 'hey, hey, hey', and 'get out of here', which he likely heard around the pool.[39]

Weddell seals under the ice.

Harbour seals are also said to be fond of the sounds made by human musicians. William Dunbar recounted his experience to the nineteenth-century naturalist William Lizars:

In walking along the shore in the calm of a summer afternoon, a few notes of my flute would bring half a score of them within thirty or forty yards of me; and there they would swim about, with their heads above water, like so many black dogs, evidently delighted with the sounds. For half an hour, or, indeed, for any length of time I chose, I could fix them to the spot; and when I moved along the water edge, they would follow me with eagerness, like the Dolphins who, it is said, attended Arion, as if anxious to prolong the enjoyment. I have frequently witnessed the same effect when out on a boat excursion. The sound of the flute, or of a common fife, blown by one of the boatmen, was no sooner heard, than half a dozen would start up within a few yards, wheeling round us as long as the music played, and disappearing, one after another, when it ceased.[40]

The twentieth-century British author Rowena Farre shared her childhood home with a particularly musical harbour seal named 'Lora'. Not only did Lora learn the 'blow-suck' method that enabled her to play the mouth organ and a toy trumpet, but she enjoyed singing:

> An unfortunate result of the singing lessons I had given her was that now, whenever Aunt or I would play the piano, Lora, were she in the vicinity, would immediately lift her head and wail fortissimo. It is well nigh impossible to struggle through a Brahms sonata with a seal singing at the top of its voice.[41]

FEASTING AND FASTING

It is reported that the Caspian seal is so fond of sculpin that during the fish run, some seals may actually gorge themselves to death.

Raymond Sheppard, 'Lora', illustration for Rowena Farre, *Seal Morning* (1957).

Depending on species and habitat, seals dine not only on fish of all types, but on squid and other cephalopods, crustaceans and krill – and some even feast on warm-blooded prey, including other seals. Leopard seals are perhaps the most feared by their fellow pinnipeds, and with reason, for they will chase and eat the young of almost all the other Antarctic species.[42] Some male leopard seals specialize in 'penguin hunts', but they are not the only seals who relish the taste of fowl. Harbour seals have been recorded sneaking up on ducks and other sea birds:

> That it aspires to more epicurean tastes is evidenced by its occasional capture of sea-birds . . . An eye-witness of this pastime relates an instance as observed by him on the Scottish coast. 'While seated on the bents,' he writes, 'watching a flock of herring gulls . . . I was startled by their jerking high in the air, and screaming in an unusual and excited manner. On no previous occasion have I ob-served such a sensation in a gull-hood . . . The excitement was explained by a Seal . . . showing above the water with a herring gull in his mouth. On his appearing the gulls became ferocious, and struck furiously at the Seal, who disappeared with the gull in the water.'[43]

More recently, a harbour seal off the same coast was observed stalking, capturing and eating an eider duck, suggesting these 'epicurean tastes' have been passed along for generations.[44]

Seals build reserves of blubbery fat in preparation for long periods of fasting. Many seals fast during the breeding season, the females in order to protect and nurse their pups, and the males in order to protect the females and defend their territories. Despite her fast, a mother seal can provide amazingly rich milk to her pup during an intensive nursing period.[45] In the shortest lactation period of any mammal, hooded seal pups will nearly double their birth weight in just four to five days. Their mothers will lose at least 35 kg (77 lb), producing milk that is 45–65 per cent fat. The shortness of the lactation period is related to the nursery environment for these northern seals. Pagophilic seals haul out on pack ice, which is often unstable and certainly very cold. Many pups are born with no blubber, and although their fur is an amazingly good insulator, they need to add a fat layer as soon as possible. Antarctic seals and those living on land-fast ice can afford to nurse for a number of weeks, before they too must leave their now bloated pups and return to the sea. Even seals that breed on beaches and rocky shores are amazingly efficient nursers. Marianne Riedman, who studied northern elephant seals, was astounded by the efficiency of energy transfer from mother to offspring. By the end of the four-week lactation period, a mother elephant seal would have lost 42 per cent of her initial body weight, providing 138 kg (304 lb) of milk to her greedy pup:

A harbour seal nursing her pup at Point Lobos, California.

Well-fed elephant seal pups on South Georgia Island.

> The enormous transfer of energy from mother to pup is obvious to anyone who simply watches an elephant seal mother-pup pair from birth to weaning: the mother gradually 'deflates' while her pup balloons into a little barrel of blubber.[46]

In the course of her study of these self-sacrificing females, Riedman did more than simply watch. She invented a vacuum pump 'milking stick' to draw samples of milk from the nearly one-ton seal: sneaking up to the unsuspecting female, Riedman latched on to the exposed teat until the mother realized that this strange apparatus was no baby seal, and charged the researcher. Riedman also sampled this super rich milk herself, anticipating a creamy treat but discovering a waxy mass with a 'nutty blandness', excellent for seals but less appealing to humans.[47] The milk is over 54 per cent fat and contains very little water, ensuring that the mother does not suffer overly from dehydration during her nursing fast.

Males also undergo prodigious fasts during the breeding season, particularly elephant seals, who defend their territories and harems for up to three months. Scientists have speculated that the stones found in their stomachs (gastroliths) may quell to some extent the pangs of hunger caused by the contraction of stomach muscles during prolonged fasting, which may account for the 35 kg (77 lb) of stones found in one southern elephant seal. Other seal species also 'eat' rocks. Sealers thought that the stones served as 'ballast' to help fat seals sink, but researchers now suggest that gastroliths may help grind up parasitic worms that can infest seals, or serve to break up food that has been swallowed whole, much as pebbles do in the gizzards of birds.

Once a mother seal has given all she can to her pup, she abruptly abandons the nursery and heads for the open sea to replenish the body mass she has lost. Weaners, or young seals that have finished nursing and have ballooned to a maximum weight, will in turn begin to fast once their mothers leave them, in some cases living off fat stores for up to three months while they learn life skills in shallow waters. According to the nineteenth-century fish merchant Michael Carroll, harp seals deliberately gave birth on the ice close to shore to provide maximum advantage for their orphaned pups:

> [Harp seals] found about Newfoundland will at all times endeavor to whelp as near the shore as possible, because instinct teaches them that the nearer the rocks the shallower the water, so that when they abandon their young ones the little creatures will see the bottom so as to enable them to procure their food.

Unfortunately for the 'little ones', all too often the sea ice would begin to raft up against the shore, and 'thousands upon thousands of them are also chopped into piece-meal'.[48]

Some seals also fast during the moulting season, when certain species shed their coats. About the middle of April, four to five weeks after the birth of the young, harp seals haul out on the ice and scrub themselves against the rough surfaces to dislodge their old and evidently itchy skin. The Germans called this the period of *Hautkrankheit* (skin-sickness),[49] and it appears to be a period of great discomfort for seals, when their new skin is delicate and easily damaged:

> If the day be warm, the skin on the back is sure to be sunburnt, so much so, that you can tear it off with your fingers; they will remain on the ice to be killed when once they get sunburnt rather than go in the water. When they do get in the water they will cry with pain.[50]

Elephant seals in particular undergo catastrophic moults. For a period of several weeks they haul out on the shore, and sealers would attest that each animal loses half its fat: 'indeed, it sometimes becomes very thin, and is then called a "slim-skin"'.[51]

We most frequently observe seals when they share our terrestrial habitat, and until recently their natural history comprised what was observed in captivity or in colonies on land, what sailors and sealers saw at sea or on ice, and what taxonomists deduced from the few specimens in museums. From his descriptions, it would seem that Aristotle, the Greek philosopher and naturalist, had the opportunity to observe what must have been monk seals close at hand:

> The seal is an amphibious animal: that is to say, it cannot take in water, but breathes and sleeps and brings forth on dry land . . . It is viviparous by immediate conception and brings forth its young alive, and exhibits an after-birth and all else just like a ewe . . . It conducts its young ones, when they are about twelve days old, over and over again during the day down to the sea, accustoming them by slow degrees to the water. It slips down steep places instead of walking, from the fact that it cannot steady itself by its feet.[52]

On land, as Aristotle noted, the seal is clumsy, 'a kind of imperfect or crippled quadruped' that must slither over the ground.[53] Joel Asaph Allen, a nineteenth-century American naturalist, described seal progression on land as 'mainly accomplished by a wriggling, serpentine motion of the body', yet he also revealed in his collected accounts that seals were in fact quite adept at terrestrial locomotion.[54] He relates the story of a young Swedish seal, who covered considerable terrain before being killed:

> During the winter of 1829 . . . a young Gray Seal took to the land . . . and finally entered the hamlet of Andersbo, situated about three (English) miles from Dannemora (the celebrated iron-mines), where it was overtaken by its pursuers and killed. The peregrinations of this Seal are believed to have occupied nearly a week, it being, as is imagined, without nourishment of any kind; and during which period it must have gone over at least thirty (English) miles of country.[55]

Snow and ice help a seal 'toboggan' along, and both ribbon seals and the Antarctic crabeater seals can match a human sprinter at speeds of up to 25 km per hour (15.5 mph).

Earlier natural history writers tended to emphasize what seals gave up when they left the land, but new ways of following the seal into the deep have encouraged greater appreciation of what they have gained. Victor Scheffer noted that in comparison to land mammals, seals are more sociable, longer-lived and more mobile, characteristics many humans would envy. Life at sea encouraged the tendency to form aggregations, particularly at breeding times, and to follow the currents and the ice. Living on the ice or remote islands, safe from most predators (other than the human) and disease, seals have little to fear, and they enjoy long lives and multi-generational companionship. If food should fail, or sites become too perilous, seals are eminently mobile, slipping into the waters and disappearing from human gaze. Researchers in Erebus Bay in Antarctica feared for the future of a group of Weddell seals blocked from their traditional breeding ground by a giant iceberg. Their fears were groundless, for when the iceberg melted, the same seals returned and flourished.[56] The scientists at Erebus knew they were indeed the former residents because since the 1960s they had been tagging, censusing, filming and tracking the Weddell seals who called the bay home. New technologies have permitted scientists to follow the seals where earlier naturalists could not dream of going – into the sea. In the name of science the seals have worn waterproof backpacks full of instruments, and sported time-depth recorders and video cameras epoxied to their heads and temperature monitors attached to their flippers. What researchers have learned has revealed glimpses into a life so foreign, it is almost unimaginable to those who enter the water with trepidation.

Once released from the constraints of breeding, nursing or moult, most seals range widely. In two migration seasons, northern elephant seal males might travel up to 21,000 km (13,000 miles) in 250 days at sea. It had always been difficult to find and track these seals after they had left the nurseries or moulting sites; not surprising, once tracking data revealed that northern elephant seals spent 86 per cent of their time underwater. They do not even seem to sleep, diving over 60 times per day to depths that would crush most mammals, and staying below on average 20–24 minutes. During their deep, deep dives, their lungs collapse, their hearts slow and they store oxygen in the nearly black tissues of their muscles and in their thick blood. Weddell seals also dive to the dark ocean bottom below the Antarctic ice, and often remain in the relative comfort of the polar sea, with its constant temperature of −1.8°C (29°F).

Even with their multiple adaptations, seals remain air breathers, and must surface several times an hour to gulp a lungful of air through a breathing hole or tidal crack in the sea ice. Not all seals dive so deeply, but several range more widely. Harp and hooded seals follow the pack ice south in winter, returning north in the spring. These annual migrations have been followed for centuries by human observers, who have not needed sophisticated tracking devices to see the vast herds:

Satellite transmitter placed on the head of a cow elephant seal in Antarctica.

As the severity of the weather increases it is evident that, like swallows, an instinctive movement must commence, communicated to and understood by the whole family, like a masonic sign . . . At length the frost commences, and the army is set in motion . . . the vanguard . . . invariably consists of small detachments of from half a dozen to a score of Seals . . . The main body is now at hand, and during the greater part of the next two days one continuous, uncountable crowd is constantly in sight. The whole procession coasts along at no great distance from the shore, presenting to an eye-witness a most extraordinary scene. In all quarters, as far as the eye can carry, nothing is visible but Seals.[57]

Harp seals may travel up to 5,000 km (3,107 miles) on this yearly trek. Grey seals and Hawaiian monk seals will also travel long distances into the open ocean, and even harbour seals, who delight in their home beaches, will range up to 300 km (186 miles) into unfamiliar waters. The ease with which seals slide through the sea, their enviable comfort in what is to most people an unnatural element, has led those who live near the seals to see them as both cohabitants of the coasts, and uncanny spirits of a world they cannot begin to imagine.

2 Seals and People

In his landmark analysis of domestication, Francis Galton used the seal as an example of an animal that, while easily tamed, could not be domesticated. Galton described a number of conditions required for domestication, such as hardiness, fondness for the human species and desire for comfort. All these conditions a seal might meet, but Galton also insisted that domesticated animals be useful. Galton described a young seal adopted by a family in the Shetlands. Appreciated as a charming pet and loved for 'human ways', in the end the seal was abandoned, judged to be of no utility and too troublesome to keep.[1] As a farmer in New Zealand who had also bagged a seal discovered: 'He cannot make it milk his cows it won't bark at tramps and if kept in close confinement . . . it is liable to emit an unhealthy odour.'[2] Despite classical references to the briny flocks of Proteus, no one has yet succeeded in corralling the great seal herds.[3]

Seals can, however, be tamed, and they do show considerable fondness for human company. Baron Cuvier, observing a 'marbled' or harbour seal in nineteenth-century Paris, remarked that:

> Except in some Monkeys, I have never known any wild animal which was more easily tamed, or attached itself more strongly. When it first came to the Jardin des Plantes, it endeavoured to escape, when I wished to touch it; but,

in a very few days, all its apprehensions vanished: it had
discovered my intentions, and rather desired my caresses
than feared them.[4]

Cuvier was equally impressed by the behaviour of what he
thought was a young 'Hare of the Sea' (*Phoca leporina*, now named
the bearded seal):

I had this animal under my care for a considerable time,
and it was easily tamed . . . He was peculiarly attached to
the old woman who had care of him. He soon came to
recognise her at the greatest distance it was possible for
him to espy her; he kept his eye upon her so long as she
was in sight, and ran to her as soon as she approached his
enclosure. It may be suspected that hunger augmented
his apparent affection.[5]

Rowena Farre also remarked on her seal's devotion to the human
family:

Lora, even if she did absent herself for a day, always returned
home to sleep. No dog could have been more faithful or
devoted to her human companions than she was.[6]

Their relative docility and expressed fondness for human
company has had a number of consequences for seals. The tame
seal Galton observed was eventually shot while basking, un-
afraid of the hunter and his gun. Other seals, easily captured,
have served a spectrum of human needs, from amusement to
companionship.

Not only could seals be tamed, but in his *Natural History* Pliny the Elder noted that 'they are susceptible . . . of training'. The idea of the 'trained seal' is now so common that the phrase has entered the English language as a cliché for someone who follows orders obediently (though that is not necessarily the case for the real seals). Through training, a tame seal could be rendered 'useful', in the sense that it could be taught to perform for human pleasure. The seals that Pliny watched in first-century Rome were apparently taught 'with their voice, as well as by gestures . . . to salute the public; when called by their name, they answer with a discordant kind of grunt'.[7] These seals were most likely the now endangered Mediterranean monk seal, and the Roman enthusiasm for the animal show may well have begun their long decline to near-extinction. Wild seals were captured and brought to Rome as combatants in battles that usually went poorly for the seals. A contemporary of Pliny, the Roman poet Calpurnius Siculus, described a day at the circus, in which not only were the crowds delighted with the beasts of the forest, but they watched with enthusiasm as the bears of the sea (presumably polar bears imported from the north) battled the local 'sea-calves'. A century later the poet Oppian, who wrote a celebrated treatise on fish and fishing, gave the advantage to the 'dread-eyed Seal', before whom he claimed the 'maned bears' of the land tremble.[8] Seals continued to perform in Rome well into the modern era. According to the sixteenth-century Swiss naturalist Konrad Gesner, who collected all the animal sightings of his age, they also appeared in cities and towns throughout Europe, hauled about by travelling showmen, like the one that Ulisse Aldrovandi, the naturalist of Bologna, encountered in 1638:

In this town I saw a marine calf with an itinerant show by which it had been dragged throughout the whole of Europe, trained at the name of its master Christianus to give I know not what voice as if afflicted by joy, but on the contrary, with any other name, be it Turk or heretic, to remain quite silent.[9]

These unfortunate performing seals, either Mediterranean monk seals or common harbour seals, were transported in crates lined with straw, provided with a wooden tub filled with fresh or salted water, and placed on exhibit as monsters of the deep, perhaps mermaids, or even just as rarities to those who lived far from the sea. Many seals wasted away on their travels, refusing to eat and dying of disease and maltreatment. Those that did survive proved the adaptability and intelligence of their kind, as numerous accounts reveal. A female seal appearing in a travelling show in Nîmes in 1777 not only obeyed the voice of her master, but blew out a candle with the breath from her nostrils, and lived, as a proper French seal, on eels. Others learned a repertoire of tricks – barking on command, the 'rollover' and the 'flipper handshake'.[10]

Cuvier saw the seal's performing abilities as evidence of phocine intelligence:

It would be a mistake to suppose that Seals are deficient in intelligence; on the contrary, it is certain that they have more than most quadrupeds, more even than dogs originally.[11]

Performing seals could be taught like dogs to respond to their names, but unlike dogs who might answer to 'Spot', 'Fido' or 'Blackie', the seals were usually given human names. What the Roman circus trainers or Christianus called their seals has

A flyer for the Learned Seals at the Boston Aquarial Gardens.

The Aquarial Gardens

THE LEARNED SEALS.

☞ This intensely interesting Exhibition has lately received very important additions, namely,

A LIVING PELICAN, from the Gulf of Mexico.

That rare and interesting animal, the AGOUTI, from Para.

A pair of live OPOSSUMS, from Georgia.

A Magnificent living specimen of the AMERICAN GOLDEN EAGLE.

A pair of splendid AMERICAN HORNED OWLS, &c. &c.

The MARBLED SEALS astonish and delight every one by their wonderful intelligence; they readily shake hands and bow to their friends, take a bath at the suggestion of their keeper, go through the manual exercise as seen in the cut above, and one is now taking lessons on the hand organ and exhibits remarkable proficiency.

The LIVING ALLIGATOR and all the great variety of Fish in the Glass Tanks entrances the lover of Natural History.

Also to be seen, the DEN OF SERPENTS, which contains within its transparent walls a large family of Serpents, some of which are over twelve feet in length.

Aquarial Gardens, 21 Bromfield Street.

CUTTING & BUTLER, Proprietors.

ADMITTANCE 25 CTS. CHILDREN UNDER 10 YEARS, 15 CTS.

not been recorded, but a young seal on exhibition in London in 1859 answered to the name of 'Jenny'. She was advertised as the 'Talking and Performing Fish',[12] and could roll over, stand on her tail, clasp her flippers in prayer and even give her keeper a 'kiss', but according to the Victorian naturalist Frank Buckland, her conversation was very limited:

> Understanding the orders given, she uttered what I believe to be her natural cry, and which, when the spectator is told means 'mamma' or 'papa' is certainly very like those infantile words. The papers stated she could 'call John' but she did not get further than 'mamma' or 'papa,' nor, indeed, is she ever likely to be made to improve upon her own natural language, which, luckily for the proprietor, may be said to resemble our own, as regards these two simple words. A good parrot, magpie or starling would beat the 'fish' hollow at talking.[13]

At the same time on the other side of the Atlantic, Fanny and Ned, a pair of 'educated' though non-talking harbour seals, performed at the Boston Aquarial Gardens. The two seals had been captured in Maine and 'were then about three months old'. James Cutting, their trainer and founder of the Gardens, recognized their potential as a novel attraction and 'proceeded to half-civilize a pair of seals which he soon exhibited as "learned" individuals who had graduated at an amphibious university'. By all accounts he orchestrated a remarkable postgraduate performance from Fanny and Ned:

> the queer pupils did credit to the enthusiastic and ingenious professor, for they played on a hand-organ, turning the crank with their fore-flippers, made bows to the gentlemen,

threw kisses to the ladies, and seemed to do everything but speak. Never had there been such an attraction in Boston before, and to see the 'learned seals,' Fanny and Ned, strings of carriages daily disgorged their contents at the foot of the long staircase in Bromfield Street.[14]

While he may not have talked, Ned was handy with a gun, as befitted a seal of the new frontier, and an 1860 advertisement shows him toting a rifle beneath his flipper, presumably to protect his lady. 'Learned seals' were also popular on the continent, but seemingly in short supply, at least in Paris. The circus performers of the Champs-Élysées were seals in name only, being played by young men dressed in sealskin, who after two or three years of being submerged in water for several hours a day were forced to give up the trade on account of their rheumatism.[15]

Trained seals, whether real or artificial, were a staple of the circus. While the traditional circus seal is most often a sea lion, seals have also performed, though with less success, under the big top.[16] Perhaps the most famous performing seal was one that did few tricks, but whose presence alone was a spectacle. What could be more awe-inspiring than a giant of the animal kingdom – an elephant of the sea? The elephant seal was difficult to capture, impossible to transport and more valuable to sealers reduced to a barrel of oil. Nevertheless, by the early twentieth century this giant seal became a circus star, aptly named 'Goliath'. Just as Jumbo applied to both specific and generic elephants, Goliath had become the name for 'sea elephants', thanks to a short story entitled 'The Largest Pet in the World', which appeared in the popular American children's magazine *St Nicholas* in 1883. Tom Barrow was a young sailor on the sealer *Mary Ann*, and known on ship for his gentle ways. On arrival in South Georgia, he could not bring himself to club his first seal:

'What's the matter, Tom? Can't ye kill 'im?' asked one of the sailors, as he passed where Tom stood. 'Here, let me show ye.' With which words he raised his club, and was about to bring it down on the nose of the animal, when Tom caught his arm, and exclaimed: 'No, no, Jack; I can't let ye. It goes agin me so, it does. See the tears in his eyes.' 'Ho, ho!' shouted Jack; 'they all does it. Ye'll soon get used to it. Here! let me.' 'No, no; now don't ye! I think, Jack,' he added, shamefacedly, 'I'll just tell the captain I'm not up to this work.'

Tom's refusal made him a victim of his shipmates' teasing, until they realized that

Tom was making a pet of the gigantic seal! Every morning and night he carried fish, as much as could be spared (and there was always plenty) to his Goliath, as he called the seal.[17]

Goliath repaid Tom's attentions with affection, allowing him to ride on his back like a marine cowboy, as an accompanying illustration showed. The story ended in tragedy, as it did for most of the seals of South Georgia, with Goliath's death at the hands of Tom's disgruntled shipmate. John R. Coryell, the moralizing author of this sad tale, lamented the near-extinction of these affable animals, though he noted that two could be seen at the Philadelphia Zoological Gardens.

The two young sea elephants in Philadelphia were on display until the 1890s. In 1910 two more sea elephants appeared at the Hagenbeck Zoo in Hamburg.[18] John Ringling of the Ringling Brothers Circus knew a good thing when he saw it. In the 1920s he purchased the two Hamburg seals, took them back to America, and named them, of course, Goliath I and Goliath II. They were of prodigious bulk, Goliath II weighing over 2,268 kg (5,000 lb), and according to a newspaper report, they were prodigiously ugly: 'Insanely popeyed, ponderously oozy, hideously fierce of tusk and whisker, a full-grown sea-elephant suggests some monstrous abortion of the animal kingdom's primal urge.' Neither Goliath I nor II was required to tote a rifle or clap flippers. It was enough that the monster sea elephant – 'the Greatest Sea Monster Ever Exhibited Alive' – was carried around the arena either on a wagon hauled by eight Clydesdale horses, or in a motor truck, 'snorting like thunder, gulping fat herring by the barrel'. The Goliaths were also reported to move under their own power, which, according to Ringling's publicist, 'was the equivalent of a steamroller operating on one cylinder'.[19] The Goliaths' winter home was a 'corral' in the waters of Sarasota Bay in Florida, and there Goliath I met his end when reportedly attacked by either a shark or an octopus that found a way into his enclosure.

The giant elephant seal Goliath at the Vincennes Zoo, Paris, 1936.

Seals at Asahiyama
Zoo, Japan.

Rescued by his keeper Emil, he later succumbed to his wounds,
to be replaced in the circus by Goliath II, until the latter's demise
in 1932.[20]

Although they no longer lumbered around the ring, elephant
seals remained feature attractions at zoos in Europe and America. 'Roland' of the Berlin Zoo was the star of a 1931 short film
that claimed 'He is the leader of the "Eat more Fish" Brigade'
(he ate 70 kg (154 lb) of fish every day).[21] Yet another Goliath
entertained at the Vincennes Zoo before the Second World War,
and in the 1960s at Stuttgart an elephant seal named Tristan
raised his ponderous bulk to beg for fish, perhaps his only trick.

Seals continue to be popular attractions at zoos and marine
parks throughout the world, the majority being harbour and
grey seals. Zoos and aquaria exhibit seals born in captivity and
provide refuge for injured and rescued animals that cannot be

Watching the seals watching us, at the Hel Marine Station, a research facility at the University of Gdansk Institute of Oceanography, Poland.

returned to the sea.[22] Most accredited zoos provide enriched environments for their captives, and use them as 'spokeseals' for environmental conservation and education about marine mammals.[23] Zoos and marine mammal centres are very aware of the power of the seal's 'baby face' to attract interest and support. Unlike many other mammals, seals do reproduce in captivity, and a website dedicated to the 'zoo-borns' encourages institutions and individuals to share their pictures of newborn animals, the 'conservation ambassadors' for their wild cousins. Seals feature prominently, because they are, as one enthusiastic report put it, 'insanely cute!' The grey seal pup born at the National Zoo in Washington in February 2014 is reported to be 'just oozing with cuteness' in a video posted online.[24] And while not cute in the traditional sense, Maruko, a southern elephant seal, has been 'the guest' and great attraction of Futami Sea Paradise in Japan since 1989. 'Maru' in Japanese is 'round' or 'rounded', a not-inappropriate name for the Goliath of seals.[25]

FRIENDSHIPS

Baron Cuvier remarked on how quickly seals became habituated to human company at the Jardin des Plantes, Paris. So readily do some seals become tamed, he said, that they appear to 'finally forget their former independence, and, by a second nature, enjoy their society with men'.[26] There are in fact many stories of seals who forsake their own and find a home with humankind, either through intention or by accident. In some cases these associations are of such an intimate nature that they move beyond the traditional human–pet relationship into the realm of an inter-species friendship, and one in which the individuality and independence of the animal partner is never in doubt. Common or harbour seals have inspired great affection in those people they have chosen to befriend. When Lora returned to the sea, Rowena Farre mourned the loss of the 'closest and most intelligent animal friend I have ever had'.[27]

So fond was George Swallow of Hoover, the famous 'Talking Seal', that he had Hoover's portrait engraved on his headstone next to his own. George and Alice Swallow had adopted Hoover as an orphan in 1971 and soon discovered his particular talent. In the wild, seals have a remarkable range of vocalizations – moaning, singing, whistling, grunting and roaring. Hoover also spoke English, or at least a surprising number of phrases, in what anthropologist Terrence Deacon described as a 'sort of a down-east, old-salt accent', likely learned from his intimate relationship with his first caregivers. Hoover didn't move his mouth to 'talk', but in his permanent home at the New England Aquarium he would chuckle and startle visitors with 'Hello there', 'how are ya' or 'get down'. Deacon recounts 'stumbling across Hoover while walking near the aquarium one evening. He thought a guard was yelling at him ("Hey! Hey! Get outta there!")'.[28] When George visited Hoover at the aquarium, the seal would answer not to his name but to George's affectionate 'Hey, stupid!'[29]

The New England Aquarium, where Hoover lived for fourteen years, insisted that he was the most famous seal in the world, having been featured on American radio and television, and certainly the only seal to have an obituary in the *Boston Globe*.[30] Hoover shared the spotlight at the Aquarium, however, with an equally famous seal named Andre. Like Hoover, Andre was a Maine harbour seal, adopted into a human family at a very young age. Harry Goodridge was a part-time scuba diver, with 'an itch for submarine companionship'.[31] He had always been fascinated by seals, since a boyhood encounter with an old bull seal:

> He rose up suddenly just beyond the grasses and, droplets glistening on his patriarchal whiskers, bade me a pleasant good morning. I felt a tingling thread of communion running between us. It was my feeling then and later that seals are wise and friendly creatures. I had the curious sense that they wished to be friends.[32]

The Goodridge family home was a menagerie of pigeons, squirrels, guinea pigs, rabbits, beagles and Reuben the Robin. Harry Goodridge insisted that as all the children had names, 'so did our feral wards': 'A name is an acknowledgement of individuality. Reuben was a bird; he was also a robin; and more specifically and meaningfully, he was Reuben.'[33] In the summer

of 1961, Goodridge met Andre: 'he came to me out of the sea that
day . . . as a dog comes to his friend and master, freely and without fear.'[34] Goodridge and his family nursed, weaned and trained
the young seal, not to exploit Andre or entertain an audience
(though Andre ended up as the most popular summer attraction
at the waterfront of Rockport, Maine), but to prove that the harbour seal was in fact trainable. Andre was a natural, and his
repertoire of behaviours and his antics also made him a star
performer at the New England Aquarium, where he eventually

spent his winters. Andre returned for the summers to Rockport and the Goodridges, and though too big to continue to live in their house, he remained around the waterfront as the 'Honorary Harbor Master'. He snoozed on boats and lobster traps, tolerated by the local community, and on one momentous occasion, according to what a local informant told Goodridge, was seen disporting himself very publicly on a marina float with a 'nubile lady':

> I got some news for you, Harry, and you better believe it! A few days back, I came down as I do to look things over. Well, sir, I looked down over the seawall and there's Andre with a female, he was topside, – huggin' her with his flippers and puttin' it right to her. A one-night stand, I suppose. Haven't seen the lady since.[35]

Seals had not always been so appreciated by local residents. In 1900 the state of Maine established a bounty on harbour seals, and in the five years until the bounty was rescinded, town clerks paid out over $25,000, at the rate of one dollar per nose.[36] In Rockport, Andre was in little danger. As one local official put it, 'We don't even consider him a wild animal – he's more of a town character.'[37] Harry and Andre's story became a book in 1975 and a movie in 1994. Despite Goodridge's insistence on the intelligence and trainability of the harbour seal, Andre was played on screen by a sea lion, the epitome of the trained seal, and Andre's despised rival for popular acclaim at the Aquarium.

The naturalist Ronald Lockley, another acute observer of seals, also raised an orphaned common seal, whom he named Diana. He described Diana as an affectionate member of the family, with a degree of intelligence Lockley felt exceeded that of a house dog, and a love for human companionship. Lockley later closely studied wild grey seals, and felt it was more difficult 'to make

Grey seals at the Cornish Seal Sanctuary, near Gweek, Cornwall.

friends' with grey seal pups, though whether this was a matter of individual temperament or specific difference is unclear.[38]

Ken Jones, known as the 'Seal Doctor', who established a seal sanctuary and hospital in Cornwall, felt that 'every seal has a character of its own, not one the same as the other.' He recounted experiences of amazingly friendly seals, particularly one of his first surviving grey seal orphans, Simon, who had a 'wonderful temperament', and whom Jones regarded as a close friend.[39] It is no surprise that their human companions cannot help but call the seals who befriend them by human names.[40]

LEARNING ABOUT SEALDOM

Harry Goodridge mused on the fruits of his long friendship with Andre:

> I wondered what he had learned in his . . . years of asso-
> ciation with man. Not much, I concluded. On the other

hand, what I had learned about sealdom from my friend Andre was of value beyond price.[41]

Understanding the life of the seal, despite affection and even companionship, has been a challenge for researchers. In *Halic: The Story of a Gray Seal*, Ewan Clarkson insisted on the unknowability of seal-kind:

> Yet the gulf which separated Halic from the world of man was infinitely wider and deeper than the Sound . . . The seals had renounced any claim they might have had on the land, and asked only to be left in peace. They are uncommunicative, and their minds remain as difficult to fathom as the deep waters that lie beyond the Continental shelf.[42]

Ronald Lockley, on the other hand, dove more deeply into the mysteries of sealdom. In 1941 Lockley was on a wartime reconnaissance mission along the Welsh coast when he discovered the cove of the Godir, a Welsh word for 'the wilderness along the edge of the sea'. Here he counted more than 100 grey seals, 'most of them peacefully asleep, a few mildly quarrelling, a few yawning and stretching and scratching as humans do on waking'. He spent several hours of his 'secret official business' for the Royal Navy watching seals, and three years later returned 'to the Godir, to its assembly of seals, and its sweet human loneliness and austere loveliness'.[43] Camping on the shingle beach under his upturned *curragh* (a large coracle), he lived for almost a month next to the grey seal cows and calves, whose trials he observed with the eye of a naturalist and friend. He named them Mavis and Maude, Nun and Novice, Blackbird and Curragh, Caesar and Brutus, and he had a special place for the orphaned waif Billy, 'a wretched, thin-looking male', named after a tame seal he had known as a boy in Cardiff. For several weeks he observed the seals, noting the tender relationships between mother and child, recording their movements, weighing the young calves, and listening to their moans and cries. He watched how Novice learned to swim under the watchful eyes of his mother, how 'his round handsome face with huge liquid brown eyes would wrinkle with seal's laughter as he sported alone in the sunlit sapphire of the shallow pools'.[44] Lockley was an experienced naturalist, but he fell easily into the rhythm of the seals' lives. He was especially struck by the behaviour of the seals in spring and returned again and again to observe 'this incessant play, this waltzing, this endless spring water-dancing'. As a scientist, he speculated on this behaviour, but as a companion of seals, he was enchanted by the dances: 'waltz and figure-of-eight and minuet and shallow-dive in close embrace,

The seal tango, photograph by Robert Bailey.

face to face or pick-a-back, for over an hour; with little breaks for kissing'.[45] His observations led to new understanding of the life cycle and breeding habits of grey seals, but he also gained an envious appreciation of the 'storm-swift joy of the free wild seals', which later resulted in a very different account of sealdom and its attractions for the human heart.[46]

While Lockley observed seals in the wild, Terrie Williams, Director of the Marine Mammal Physiology Project at the University of California in Santa Cruz, learned a great deal from her relationship with an individual seal in her lab. Her research group studies the physiology and performance of otters, sea lions, seals, dolphins and whales, but her most celebrated subject has been a seal named, prosaically, KP2. In 2009 Williams was working with Weddell seals in the Antarctic when she received the offer of a Hawaiian monk seal orphan for the lab. These are among the most endangered marine mammals in the world, restricted to the Pacific archipelago. With just over 1,000 left in the wild, Williams's concern about losing even one individual translated into her struggle to save what turned out to be a most singular seal. Like the other animals at her lab, KP2 was destined to become his species' representative, the 'spokeseal' to a human population that Williams felt had 'overwhelmed nature's capacity to heal'.[47] Unlike the harbour and grey seals, monk seals have a reputation for disdaining human company. Little wonder, given the species' history of conflict with people in the Mediterranean, the Caribbean and in the waters around the Hawaiian islands. Local fishermen considered them 'invasive species', though the seals had colonized the islands long before the arrival of Polynesian settlers. Half-eaten fish, torn nets and fouled gear, plus the seals' wary avoidance of human company, did not endear them to islanders. But monk seals are also individuals, and KP2, or Kauai Pup 2 – named in rigorously objective fashion by the scientific observers of his birth – revealed

a nature anything but introspective and solitary. Abandoned at birth, rescued and hand-reared by a team of veterinarians and biologists in a research facility, at the age of five months he was airlifted to the island of Molokai and returned to the sea. Despite partial blindness, attributed to deprivation of the wild seal pup's best start in life, his mother's rich milk, he seemed to be adapting well to the life of a wild seal, until he rediscovered his pink boogie board. KP2 had learned to swim in the saltwater pools of the lab; his first attempts were fraught with problems until his human swimming coaches threw him a foam boogie board. The fat little seal turned out to be a natural surfer, and paddled around the pool until he could indeed swim like a seal. On Molokai, the

Hawaiian monk seal on the beach at French Frigate Shoals, Hawaii.

adolescent seal frequented the harbour of Kaunakakai, and became a favourite with the locals, slapping the water with his flipper in greeting, swimming with the children and appropriating their boogie boards. To the islanders, he became something more than a seal; like Andre, he became a 'local'. Ancient Hawaiians called his kind '*ilio holo kauai* – "the dog that runs in rough water"', but they called KP2 Hoʻailona, 'a sign from the sea'.[48]

Terrie Williams and her trainers and lab assistants developed a remarkable research partnership with KP2 ('forged in friendship and fish'),[49] helping them to unravel the constraints of physiology and metabolism that had contributed to the monk seals' imperilled status. Over fifteen million years, monk seals had adapted so completely to the warm waters of Hawaii that their ability to survive in a changing world was compromised. With overfishing and fluctuations in ocean temperatures, young monk seals had to swim further and dive deeper into cold waters to find fish, impairing the balance between metabolic calories needed to keep warm against calories ingested when they finally caught a fish. The research team also developed insight into a new and startling relationship between seals, phytoplankton and global warming. The faeces of the monk seals literally fertilize the sea, and the seals' diving and feeding stir up micronutrients, turning over the ocean, making monk seals not just fish consumers, but fish farmers. Nourished by the leavings of the seals, phytoplankton flourish, converting sunlight and carbon dioxide into food for an ocean ecosystem, and removing increasing amounts of carbon dioxide from the atmosphere. Williams concluded that:

Lieutenant Commander Marc Pickett and Lieutenant Mark Sarmek free an entangled Hawaiian monk seal at French Frigate Shoals, January 1997.

> The seals were neither invaders nor gluttons. Rather, they were ancient, honored family members who helped to create and maintain the tropical coastal ecosystem that both man and seal needed to survive.[50]

Ronald Lockley and Terrie Williams both struggled with the tension between scientific description and the lived reality of their lives with seals. Lockley attempted to revise his notes by lamplight on a seal-strewn beach. He found what he had first written pedantic, dull and uninspired: 'Yes, I had written that in the South Kensington Museum. Dry as dust stuff, but one had to begin somewhere.'[51] In the end, he abandoned his draft and began with the visceral immediacy of his observations of the seals of the Godir. Williams resisted the easy affection that might develop between animal and human companion. She always backed away, until one day after the loss of her own animal companion, she allowed herself to engage more intimately with KP2. She had prided herself on her innate ability to 'read animals'; what surprised her was KP2's ability to read her. As KP2 was being prepared for his transfer to the Waikiki Aquarium, Williams paid the big seal a visit. 'Every inch of him was handsome . . . KP2 had the longest whiskers of any seal I had ever met.' She scratched him and bade him farewell with a final warning: 'Never, ever let the others know that I used to talk to you!'[52]

VOICE OF THE OCEAN

Even if not raised by people, many seals seek human companionship. Does sealdom recognize the threat posed by human competition for space and for food? Are the seals that seek our company knowing envoys of their kind? Nelson, the one-eyed grey seal that for 25 years frequented the waters of Cornwall and eventually made the rocks in the harbour of Looe his home, is commemorated by local residents in a statue and plaque. His distinctive appearance meant that he could be easily recognized, and like Andre, become a character within the human community. Nelson died (or disappeared) in 2003, and in 2008 on his

Statue of Nelson, a bronze memorial in West Looe, Cornwall.

memorial, he was described as '"A Grand Old Man of the Sea" and a great favourite with all'. He was also recognized as 'a splendid ambassador for his species', his relationship with the local residents seemingly understood as a link to a larger community of wilder seals that had for so long been the target of human persecution. This idea of the individual animal (the familiar) acting as a go-between has a long history in the mythic relationships of animals and people. Nelson was seen not as a seal but as Nelson, somehow on our side, able to take our messages back to the others with whom we had less communication. According to the plaque, that message was one of appreciation, and Nelson, immortalized in bronze, could serve 'as a potent symbol of the rich marine environment of the area and a permanent reminder of the need for it to be cherished'.[53]

Terrie Williams and her colleagues deliberately reared KP2 to be the go-between for his endangered tribe and the human species. He became a celebrity, a star of YouTube and social media.

Carved wooden bowl in the shape of a seal, from Haida Gwaii, Canada.

He was lovingly known by many names, from 'Ho'ailona' to 'Smoodgey' and 'Mr Hoa', and he 'inspired nicknames that were as colorful as his personality. Over the years, he would be called Butthead, Honey Boy, Fish Stealer, Little Angel, Bugger, and Elvis of the Seals, depending on his mood and his audience.'[54] In 2011 Ho'ailona returned to Hawaii and the Waikiki Aquarium, but not before he had become the spokeseal for marine conservation and the 'voice of the ocean'. He even became the subject of a song, 'KP2's Rap', written by a Molokai musician, Lono:

> Monk seals are Hawaii's State Mammal,
> While topping America's endangered animals.
> Only eleven hundred of us are left,
> due to plastics, sharks, and fishermen's nets.
>
> Without creative solutions,
> some locals call monk seals 'invasive pollution'.
> We've been starved, shot, and shark thrashed;

on some island beaches we've even had our heads smashed.
Ancient history proves our critics wrong. The scientific
   evidence is strong.
No matter what they say! Who are they? We monk seals
   were born on Island waves![55]

Despite 'KP2's Rap', seals are for the most part mute in their
relationships with the human species. With some exceptions,
they have not become protagonists in literature in the ways that
rabbits, foxes, cats, dogs, horses and even birds and bats have
found a voice through human agency. Lockley's work on rabbits
(*The Private Life of the Rabbit*) inspired the epic *Watership Down*,
with its fully realized rabbit society. His work on the grey seal,
however, did not lead to the same result. Perhaps the only author
who has given seals not only a human voice, but a culture and
history, is Rudyard Kipling. Kipling was not, of course, someone
who felt distant from the animal mind. He entered into it with
glee, and his *Jungle Book* howls, warbles and hisses with the voices
of Baloo the Bear, Akela the old wolf, Darzee the tailor bird, the
evil cobras Nag and Nagina, and the triumphant mongoose Rikki-
Tikki-Tavi. Less famous perhaps, but nonetheless a sprightly character in his own right, is Kotick, the white seal. Kipling included
Kotick's story, 'The White Seal', in the first volume of *The Jungle
Book* published in 1894. Kotick is in fact a white fur seal, and while
this book does not deal with the eared seals, it is unlikely that
many of Kipling's readers made the taxonomic distinction. The
lovely seal's lullaby might be sung to all seals, eared and earless:

Oh! hush thee, my baby, the night is behind us,
And black are the waters that sparkled so green.
The moon, o'er the combers, looks downward to find us
At rest in the hollows that rustle between.

Where billow meets billow, then soft be thy pillow,
Ah, weary wee flipperling, curl at thy ease!
The storm shall not wake thee, nor shark overtake thee,
Asleep in the arms of the slow-swinging seas!

The seal Matkah's motherly advice to her wee flipperling Kotick might also apply to many of seal-kind:

You mustn't swim till you're six weeks old,
Or your head will be sunk by your heels;
And summer gales and Killer Whales
Are bad for baby seals.

Are bad for baby seals, dear rat,
As bad as bad can be;
But splash and grow strong,
And you can't be wrong.
Child of the Open Sea!

Kotick has his own voice, and speaks with a particularly British turn of phrase ('Ahem!' said Kotick. 'Good sport, gentlemen?'). Kipling also created 'a sort of very sad seal National Anthem', sung by the seals of St Paul Island that speaks to a remembered seal Arcadia:

The song of pleasant stations beside the salt lagoons,
The song of blowing squadrons that shuffled down the dunes,
The song of midnight dances that churned the sea to flame
The Beaches of Lukannon – before the sealers came![56]

Kipling's evocation of the world of the seal is part natural history, part morality tale and part epic. Kotick embodies the

84

virtues of the plucky young hero struggling against injustice and finding his special destiny. Like Mowgli or Kim, he is an outlier, a white seal in a sea of black. Unlike the other seals, he refuses to accept the annual slaughter of his people on the killing fields of Lukannon, and seeking wisdom from bird and beast he travels far and wide for five long years, to find the blessed land where seals may live without fear. He returns to his people and through skill in battle wins their trust, and leads tens of thousands from the sad beaches of Lukannon to a safe haven, fulfilling the ancient legends of his kind, his story an inspiration for seals and humans alike, and a commentary on the difficult history between seals and people.

3   Peoples of the Seal

Throughout most of their global range, seals and people live separate lives. There are, however, places where the lives of the human inhabitants are so closely woven with those of the seals that their mutual interactions are not those of individuals, but of nations. Between these peoples of the seal and the people of the sea exist long histories of conflicts, treaties, collaborations and strained relations. Around the coast of the Mediterranean – Homer's wine-dark sea – and on the grey wind- and wave-swept shores of the northern isles (the Orkneys, Shetlands and Faroe Islands); along the shore of the great polar ocean; and the scattered places of the Inuit and Greenlanders, the lives of the seals and the lives of humans have run together, both physically and spiritually. Their relations go far beyond that of hunter and hunted, venturing into terrains of surprising intimacy.

THE CHILDREN OF OCEAN

Today Mediterranean monk seals are an extremely rare sight in their ancestral home along the shores of the Mediterranean, in the Black Sea and in the waters of the North Atlantic as far south as the coast of the Western Sahara and Mauritania (the Seal Coast). In classical times, the evidence of Greek and Roman authors suggests they were hard to miss, hauled out in numbers along smooth rocks, snoozing on sandy beaches, or sheltered in the vast sea caverns described by Homer in the *Odyssey*. Homer tells the story of Menelaus and the sea god Proteus, the Old Man of the Sea, who tends his flocks of 'fat-fed' seals, counting them each morning as they doze on the shores, then lying down to sleep among them as a shepherd with his sheep. His seals are the spawn of ocean itself, 'sea-bred' ('*halosydne*') by his divine spouse, and sometimes called 'Halosydne's chickens'. Homer recounts how Menelaus, lost and seeking directions to return home after the Trojan War, was aided by Proteus' daughter, Eidothea, who devised a ruse to trick her father into giving information. Menelaus and his companions donned freshly flayed sealskins, and hid among the dozing seals to wait for Proteus. The stratagem almost proved intolerable, 'the awful reek of all those sea-fed brutes! Who'd dream of bedding down with a monster of the deep?' Fortunately for Menelaus and his companions, their helping goddess 'found the cure with ambrosia, daubing it under each man's nose – that lovely scent, it drowned the creatures' stench'.[1] Eidothea warns that her father is a shape-shifter, and to prise the information from him, Menelaus must hang on tight, no matter what terrifying shape the god assumes. From the story of Proteus and his briny flocks emerge two ideas that inform not only Greek mythology but the folklore of many European countries. There is a connection between seals and shape-shifters, and Proteus' herds with their 'awful reek' are true 'monsters of the deep'.

Shape-shifting is a recurrent theme in stories of seals and people. A sea nymph, Psamathe, whose name means 'sandy shore', turns herself into a seal in an attempt to escape an assault by Aeacus, grandson of a river god. Their offspring is Phocus ('seal'), the legendary founder of the ancient city of Phocaea, now buried under the present-day town of Foça on Turkey's Aegean coast.[2] In his *Metamorphoses*, Ovid tells of the punishment of a river-god in

Menelaus binding Proteus to force him to reveal the future; below him are monsters, possibly seals; engraving, plate 61, from *Emblems of Achilles Bocchius* (1555).

Phocis, whose grandson Apollo transforms into a seal. Alexander the Great's mother was said to be a seal, and his sister, a mermaid. Achilles' mother, Thetis Halosydne, was said to have transformed into a seal to drown Helen of Troy to avenge her son. In a folkloric retelling of the parting of the Red Sea in *Exodus*, the Pharaoh and his armies are turned into seals.[3] The idea of an easy transition from seal to man or, perhaps more often, seal to woman and back

Sébastien Slodtz, *Aristaeus and Proteus*, bronze, 1695–1700. Note the seal underfoot.

again coloured the imagination of people along the Mediterranean littoral. Young seals were 'baby-faced', while mature seals, with their bewhiskered faces, were often referred to as 'old men'. In Egypt, the seal is known as 'Sheik el Bahr', the venerable old man of the sea, and in the Balearic Islands as 'Vey mari' (the old one of the sea). Fourteenth-century maps of the Canary Islands include the Insula de Vegi mari, literally 'island of the old ones of the sea'.[4]

Ancient Greek electrum stater with a seal, attributed to Phocaea, Ionia (modern Turkey), c. 600–550 BC.

What is it in the seal's countenance that seems recognizably human? The nostrils are slits, the ears mere openings in the head, and the whiskers adorn a muzzle, not a nose. But the eyes, the windows of the soul, are large, exceedingly lustrous and expressive. Pernetty thought that the huge eyes of the elephant seal were 'the most beautiful in the world', while the Comte de Buffon saw in seals' eyes intelligence, and expressions of affection and attachment. The Orkney crofters, who lived so closely with the seal folk, averred that 'The eyes of a seal . . . are the very same as a man's eyes.'[5] And these soulful eyes can brim with tears. A weeping seal was said to portend tragedy, the animal lamenting human misfortune. Seal tears are a characteristic of their biology, and more likely to reflect distress at capture or disturbance, but weeping seems a very human attribute, as do moans and wails.[6] Greek sailors likened the particular high-pitched call of a mother monk seal to her pup to the unearthly song of the sea nymphs – the dreaded sirens that lured men to a watery doom. A Roman writer warned that 'Sea-calves lying on headlands and

'The most beautiful eyes in the world', those of a female elephant seal. Antarctica, Seal Island, 1992.

90

projecting rocks utter a kind of ominous cry . . . and whoever hears this sound, for him there is no escape, but he dies soon after.[7] Conversely, seals are lured by the calls of human offspring. So close is the cry of a human child to that of a seal that the seals are said to stray close to shore to follow the voices of children, presumably confusing them with the calls of their own young.[8] Captive female seals were also called 'women of the sea', and Aristotle noted the resemblance of their sexual anatomy to that of human females.[9] Seal mothers were praised for the care and nursing of their young, and in his celebrated tract on fishing (*Halieutica*), Oppian describes how the mother remains on land with her child for twelve days, but on the thirteenth dawn, 'she takes in her arms her young cubs and goes down into the sea glorying in her children and showing them, as it were, their fatherland'.[10]

Harbour seal mother and child, 2010.

It is hard to reconcile these charming descriptions with the classification of seals as fearsome monsters. In the otherworld

of ocean, however, they share the characteristics of the alien creatures of the sea, whom Plutarch described as 'completely lacking in amiability, apathetic, and devoid of all sweetness of disposition'.[11] Seals may be sheep in Proteus' submarine meadows, but they are also, and more sinisterly, sea-wolves and sea-bears. They savage the fishy herds and rip the fisherfolk's nets and, even worse, they devour people. The 'dread-eyed' seals were hideous corpse-eaters which after feasting on human flesh 'belched out a stream of brownish blood'.[12] Thecla, the virgin companion of Paul the Apostle, when sentenced to death in the arena, threw herself into a tank of seals, desiring to be self-baptized before she could be eaten by the ravening sea-wolves. (Divine intervention in the form of a lightning bolt kills the seals and saves the pious Thecla.) Not only do seals steal the fruits of the sea, they will even insist on sharing the fruits of the land. Classical poets saw the seal as symbol of the catastrophe that would overtake the land during a time of great floods, and Ovid lamented the submergence of pastures where graceful goats might have grazed, but now 'gross clumsy seals hauled their ungainly bulk'.[13] Seals were also said to be 'fain of the beds of mortal men', and would lumber on to shore, suck the ripe grapes from vines and plunder fruit trees.[14] On land, they moved like caterpillars, humping and shuffling, or even, to some eyes, rolling with the repellent slither of snake or worm. Aristotle described the seal on land as a crippled, misshapen creature, which 'slips down steep places instead of walking, from the fact that it cannot steady itself by its feet'.[15] In Greek folklore, St George cursed a woman who washed her baby's clothes on a holy day: 'May you become a seal and carry your swaddling clothes behind you', just as a seal drags along the shore.[16] Even a holy man like St John Chrysostom could see no beauty in the seal, and decried the glutton, disgusting in his fleshiness, who crawled 'after the manner of a seal'.[17]

There is expressed in these descriptions and comparisons a repugnance for the seal that goes beyond mere distaste at their 'awful reek'. Seals were competitors with people not only for the fish in the sea, but for choice sites on the landwash. There is something unnerving in seeing a long beach thronged with the black, glistening bodies, calling and dozing, regarding the humans as interlopers on their territory. As Aristotle recognized, 'Now there is a war against each other among all animals that occupy the same places and get their living from the same things.'[18] In the end, the monk seals of the Mediterranean did not succeed in sharing the territory of their human cohabitants. Forced out of the 'arching caverns' they preferred, and driven from the sandy beaches into the arenas and animal shows, hunted for their skins and their oil, they retreated to more and more inhospitable shores, resorting to tiny crevices and caves far from human gaze. Today they have almost disappeared entirely from our view.

Hasegawa Settan, illustration of a seal that drifted to the beach near Karatsu in the 6th year of Bunsei (1823).

Grey seals and people compete for space on the Baltic beaches of Poland.

THE SELKIE FOLK

Stories of transformation haunt human–seal relations, and nowhere are there more stories of transformation than among the northern islands of Britain. On the rugged shores of Orkney there are two kinds of seal – the common seal or 'tangfish' (sea-weed fish) of the Shetlands, fair game for any fisher, and the great grey seal, the 'selkie' or 'silkie', whose world intersects deeply with that of the islanders. Ernest Thompson Seton, the twentieth-century chronicler of the lives of the furred and feathered, said that all animal stories have a tragic end, but in the case of the seals, it is not only the beast who suffers.[19] One of the best known traditional songs of the Orkneys is 'The Great Silkie of Sule Skerry', and it tells of the sad fate of a seal-man and his half-human child. The selkie leaves the sea to find and seduce a fair human maid. Nine months later, as she rocks the cradle, the maid wonders what has happened to her child's father: 'I know not where my bairn's father is/ By land or sea does he traivel in'. Soon her selkie returns and reveals that:

> I am a man upon the land
> I am a silkie in the sea
> And when I'm far from every strand
> My dwellin 'tis on Sule Skerry

Orkney and Shetland, from the *Blaeu Atlas of Scotland*, 1654.

He promises to come again in seven years with a 'nourrice fee' or nursing fee, and claim his son. When, after seven long years, he returns to take the bairn from the maid, he places a gold chain around the child's neck so that his mother will recognize him as he swims among the waves. But the selkie also makes a dire prediction:

> An he said 'Ye'll wed a gunner guid
> An a gey guid gunner it will be
> And he'll gae oot on a May morning
> He'll shoot your son and the grey silkie'

The foolish maid weds her gunner, and with his first shot, he kills both her child and her selkie lover:

> 'Alas, alas this woeful fate
> This weary fate that's been laid on me.'
> She sobbed and sighed and bitter cried
> Her tender hert did brak in three.[20]

There is a deep current of eroticism running through the selkie tales, and the seductive male selkie is a motif in contemporary romance novels (which may also help explain the popularity of the human 'Navy Seal' bodice-ripper genre). Melanie Jackson's book *The Selkie Bride*, subtitled *An American Woman's Adventure in Scotland* and classified by the publisher as a 'Paranormal Romance', is the tale of what happens to a young widow when she opens her front door on a dark and stormy night:

> I surveyed the creature on my doorstep. He was male –
> oh, definitely male – and quite the most beautiful being
> I had ever seen. But there was also something about him

Joseph Swain, after
William Small,
'Seal Shooting',
engraving,
published in the
Cornhill Magazine,
1880.

that seemed sinister and made me feel very weak and insignificant as I stood before him. Perhaps it was the fierce black eyes or the alabaster skin, or the long hair that fell in a sleek cascade to below his shoulders. Or perhaps, most alarming of all, it was how not a drop of rain seemed to cling to him – not to his hair, not to his skin, not to the old-fashioned sark and kilt he wore most sloppily. A drop of blood ran down the side of his face, and he had an odd fur coat slung over his back.[21]

The fur coat might have given the widow a clue, for in many tales of selkies, men and women alike wear long dark coats. Cut along the belly, a seal's skin slips so easily from the carcass, it is not hard to imagine the pelt as just a covering, something that can be put on or taken off with ease. Duncan Williamson, who recorded and retold Scottish tales of the seal people, recounted how seals often appear in human society dressed in their sleek black skins. In one story, a party of seal-hunters find themselves invited to a strange feast on a deserted island:

> This tall dark man with a long dark coat said, 'Hello, come on in! Make yourselves at home!' They all came in, one by one, six of them. There was a table. There were bottles of drink, liquid laid in the middle of the table. And all those people around against the wall. Strangers they had never seen. But everyone was dressed the same way. Long dark coats.[22]

A selkie does not always wear a long coat; sometimes he wears sealskin trousers. In Scottish writer Eric Linklater's rather chilling short story 'Sealskin Trousers', a young undergraduate intent on studying biology walks along the sea cliffs to a secluded ledge that she and her fiancé had found the day before:

> But their gazebo, she perceived, was already occupied, and occupied by a person of the most embarrassing appearance. He was quite unlike Charles. He was not only naked, but obviously robust, brown-hued, and extremely hairy. He sat on the very edge of the rock, dangling his legs over the sea, and down his spine ran a ridge of hair like the dark stripe on a donkey's back, and on his shoulder-blades grew patches of hair like the wings of a bird. Unable in her disappointment to be sensible and leave at once, she lingered for a moment and saw to her relief that he was not quite naked. He wore trousers of a dark brown colour, very low at the waist, but sufficient to cover his haunches.[23]

Elizabeth recognizes the man as Roger Fairfield, a graduate of her university with an odd reputation and a talent for swimming.

The selkie, for that is the true identity of Roger Fairfield, takes Elizabeth in his arms, and tells her happily, 'You'll be the prettiest seal between Shetland and the Scillies.'[24] He grasps Elizabeth in his arms and plunges into the sea. Her fiancé, arriving moments later, finds only her clothes and her book. Out to sea he sees two seals swimming together, and hears a man's voice singing the most haunting tune he has ever heard, 'I am a Selkie in the sea . . .'

It is not only the male selkie who has a seductive charm. There are many versions of the story of the seal-woman and her human husband. As told by the American children's author Susan Cooper, the tale begins, as they all do, with a lonely man hearing beautiful music by the sea, 'like the voice of the wind'. When he goes to the shore, he sees three young women, naked and lovely, combing their long hair. At once he knows he must have one of the singing girls, but at his appearance, they startle and slip into the sea, except for one. For the young man has stolen her skin, and without it, she is doomed to live on land. No tears can move the bewitched man, and he takes the selkie-girl to be his wife, carefully hiding her skin. She is a dutiful wife, this seal-woman, bearing her husband sons and daughters, but always looking with longing to the sea. One day, her husband goes to fish, and one of her children comes to ask his mother why their father keeps an old skin in a hole in the wall. The selkie finds the skin, and runs from the house. The children follow, and see their mother slip into the sea, joining the seals who watch and wait.[25] In the kindest stories, the seal-mother returns once a year to her human family; in others, she abandons them for the kin she left behind. In an Icelandic version of the tale,

Before the woman jumped into the sea, it is reported that she said:
This I want, and yet I want it not, –

Seven children have I at the bottom of the sea,
Seven children have I as well here above.[26]

In the poem, 'Little Seal-skin', by Victorian author Eliza Keary,
the selkie simply abandons her children for the lure of the sea:

So the Fisherman had his way,
And seven years of life
Passed by him like one happy day;
But, as for his sea wife,
She sorrowed for the sea alway,
And loved not her land life.
Morning, and evening, and all day,
She would say
To herself – 'The sea! the sea!'
And at night, when dreaming,
She stretched her arms about her, seeming
To seek little Willie,
It was the sea
She would have clasped, not he –
The great sea's purple water,
Dearer to her than little son or daughter.[27]

The union of seal and human produced children of strange
character, fond of the water and good swimmers, often with telltale webs between the toes.[28] The MacCodrum clan of the Outer
Hebrides was said to have selkie blood in their veins and 'lucken'
toes resembling flippers.[29] Their peculiar heritage descended
from Ursilla, the unhappy daughter of an Orkney laird, who took
a selkie lover, and learned how to clip the webs that grew between
her children's fingers and toes:

Baubi Urquhart, great-great-granddaughter of a seal-woman, in Burravoe, Shetland, c. 1895.

And many a clipping Ursilla clipped, to keep the fins from growing together again; and the fins not being allowed to grow in their natural way, grew into a horny crust on the palms of the hands and soles of the feet. And this horny substance is seen in many of Ursilla's descendants to this day.[30]

The naturalist Ronald Lockley, intimately acquainted with seals, was moved to write a fictional erotic memoir of a young man's passion for a wild Irish girl, who also had more of the seal in her than he at first suspected:

I wanted to rub my eyes when I saw that between the long
brown fingers were webs . . . I must confess this discovery
was a shock and caused a cold feeling to pass along my
spine.[31]

The shock did not, however, abate his ardour. When at last they
finally consummate their love – in the water – he thinks, 'The
embrace of mated seals lasts long. I remembered that, even as
we drifted in the blessed peace of requited passion.'[32] Like most
selkie–human loves, the relationship did not end well, the beautiful 'Shian' abandoning both lover and child for the company
of the sleek grey seals.[33] And why would a selkie not long to return
to an Atlantis beneath the waves? When trapped in human flesh,

they would ne'er again see the city o' coral and pearl that
lies beneath the waves. And they described their city in this
song – how the sea aboon them was like a sky, but pure
blue and green, when they were hame – ten thousand times
more beautiful than the sky above the earth.[34]

There are other stories of babes found floating in the water, a
scrap of silky white sealskin beside them. These children are a gift
from the sea, often to a childless couple. But like the selkie-wife,
the sea calls them, and their human parents go to great lengths
to bind them to the land. Gioga, the daughter of the sea, is one
such child. Her mother, desperate to keep her from the seals, takes
her from their island home to the farm of kinfolk far inland,
telling them the sea is making the girl ill. But away from the sea,
Gioga pines and grows pale. Not even the murder of her selkie-
father could prevent the inevitable return of the seal-child to her
native home – 'she slipped the seal skin over her shoulders,
wrapped it around herself like a cloak, and shimmered into the

sea.'[35] Some families resorted to even more drastic measures. In Duncan Williamson's 'The Crofter's Mistake', there were two brothers: Iain, who loved the seals, and Angus, who did not. One day Iain met a beautiful woman by the shore. Soon they were married, and lived happily, but sadly Iain drowned while out fishing. Angus cared for his brother's wife, who gave birth to a child. She named her Seda after herself, and when the girl was about six years old, her mother walked to the shore and disappeared. Angus raged; the sea had taken his brother and now his brother's wife, and he was determined the sea would not claim his beloved niece. But she longed, as all selkies must, for the sea, and went often to the shore to swim among the seals. One night her uncle,

> under a drunken stupor . . . chopped off the points of her toes, and he chopped off the points of her fingers. 'Now', he said, 'you'll never join these people and go away fae me!'[36]

Sometime later, Angus rowed out to fish. The seals rose up from the sea and bit at his hands and feet, snapping off fingers and toes. He crawled home bleeding to an empty house; Seda was gone. But when Angus went down to the shore, he saw three seals: 'But the funny thing was, the young, half-grown female seal, half her flippers were gone – half her tail flipper and her front flippers were cut across.'[37] Seda had returned home.

THE ONE WHO DWELLS BELOW

In the tale of Seda is the echo of the legend of Sedna, a story of a woman and seals told throughout the Arctic, and most famously among the Inuit and Greenlanders, whose lives have been and continue to be dependent on the seal. To the Inuit of the

Central Arctic, Sedna is Sanna, the one who dwells below. She is also known as Nuliajuk, or Niviaqsi, the woman below the waves, and Talilajuq, or Nerrivik, the food dish, because she provides the animals. In Greenland she is Takanaluk Arnaluk, or Arnaquagsaq, the old woman. The story of Sedna has many variations, but the gist of the tale concerns a beautiful young woman who refuses to marry until one day a suitor comes from afar. She accepts him and travels to his country, but he is not what he seems. When her father comes to rescue her, Sedna's husband, who might be a demon but is often a bird spirit, flaps his wings to raise the waves, threatening to capsize father and daughter as they paddle away. Sedna's

Lukassie Kenojuak, *Sedna*, stone carving, *c.* 1987.

father, terrified, throws her overboard to appease the angry spirit. But Sedna, like the seal, is tenacious of life, and she clings to the side of the kayak. Finally, her father is forced to cut off her fingers, joint by joint, until she releases her grip and sinks below the waves. Her lopped-off fingers become the sea mammals – seals, walrus and whales – and she their protectress. When seals are scarce, the *angakkuq* (shaman) must dive down deep to the world below and comb and braid her long hair, which, lacking fingers, she cannot do for herself. Then Sedna releases the seals, and the Inuit have good hunting. In some stories, Sedna takes revenge on her father, calling her dogs to gnaw his feet and hands while he sleeps. Hands and feet are what the seal gives up to live in the sea. Cut off the fingers and toes and the man or woman may as well be a seal. Add hands and the seal becomes a man. (The Canadian artist William Ritchie created a lithograph showing a young seal whose front flippers have become hands, an unsettling mutability.)

Like Proteus, Sedna is the creature of transformation, sliding from seal to woman, and like the Greek god, she guards her herds. She is also the mistress of the land below, the Persephone of the Arctic, lady of the land of the dead. Sedna's tale continues to be told throughout the north in story and song, and made concrete in the prints and sculptures created by Inuit artists in Arctic Canada since the 1950s.[38] Whether sinking into the sea, braiding her hair, swimming with her seals (their heads bobbing in the waters looking like her broken finger tips) or transforming, this half fish, half woman, Sedna, is one of the great themes in Inuit art. Kenojuak Ashevak, arguably the most famous of the first generation of Inuit artists from Cape Dorset, depicted Sedna both as a fish-tailed woman – an Arctic mermaid – and a pure flippered spirit on her journey with bird spirits. A younger artist, Ningeokuluk Teevee, drew Sedna as a girl sinking down into the

L. Angatikjuaq, *Seal*, soapstone from Clyde River, Nunavut, Canada.

water, hair floating wide, blood streaming from her butchered hands. Sculptors, too, cannot resist the smooth shapes of Sedna's transformed body, woman emerging from or merged into seal, the polished stone reflecting the sheen of the seal's dark skin.[39]

Inuit storytellers also recount another tale of transformation, the story of Atarssuaq's son. Every day his father threw him into the water until he became a clever swimmer. Once he could swim like a fish, his father caught a seal and took off its skin all in one piece, and dressed his son in the skin. Then he trained his son to dive and swim under the water, and his great skill helped him to defeat his enemies, by swimming under their kayaks and pulling them down into the water until they drowned.[40] The boy, called Uxssung (ground-seal) let one man live, and this was Kiviuk, who became a famous hero, but owed his life to the boy-seal. The Scottish poet Robin Robertson describes the selkie emerging from the water and 'shrugging off his skin like a wet-suit', while a contemporary cultural hero, Bear Grylls, upends the order, and dons the skin of a dead and pungent seal to take to the cold waters off Scotland.[41]

David Thomson, in his stories of the 'Seal Folk', wrote that 'Land animals may play their roles in legend, but none, not even the hare, has such a dream-like effect on the human mind . . . the seal legend is unique.'[42] He listened to the stories the fishers and crofters of the Orkneys told, how the seals would look directly at them, how they wept, how they caressed and kissed one another. One man told him that he had heard a Shetland man say that they are 'some of the fallen angels. God threw them out'.[43] Fallen angels, drowned sailors, spirits of the dead, seals pass between human and animal, constantly in transformation, slipping in and out of their skins, and in and out of the lives of the peoples of the seal. As an Orkneyman said to David Thomson,

'It's no wonder they were thought to be like us,' he said. 'For the seals and ourselves were aye thrown together in our way o' getting a living, and everything we feel, they feel, ye may be sure o' that.'[44]

4 Hunting the Seal

The peoples of the seal are also hunters of the seal. Their ancient and complex interconnections are forged not only through legend and story, but through a tangible history of blood and flesh, skin and bone. Throughout the years seals have straddled the classifications between creature of land and creature of sea, between docile prey and deadly predator, and between companion in the hunt and hated rival. They were an important source of meat, hides, oil and remedies for the peoples with whom they shared common grounds, while they were also seen as despised competitors for marine resources. It is in this duality that the relationship between hunter and hunted continues to be defined today.

SEA COWS

In *The Compleat Angler* (1653), Izaak Walton, that most excellent student of fishy life, quoted the words of a French poet on the parallel worlds of earth and sea:

> In the waters we may see all creatures,
> Even all that on the earth are to be found,
> As if the world were in deep waters drown'd.

As also rams, calves, horses, hares, and hogs,
Wolves, urchins, lions, elephants, and dogs;
Yea, men and maids . . .[1]

The seals were likened to the cattle of the sea, or sometimes sheep or swine, grazing 'in meadows submarine'.[2] Aristotle affirmed that a seal 'looks like a cow' and Pliny said 'They make a noise which sounds like lowing, whence their name of "sea-calf".' They were seen to be of bovine dullness, and as sea-dwellers, they suffered, at least in Mediterranean cultures, from the disdain of the land-dweller for the creatures of the deep. Plutarch praised the terrestrial hunt as a 'noble sport':

> in the chase on land, brave animals give play to the courageous and danger-loving qualities of those matched against them, crafty animals sharpen the wits and cunning of their attackers, while swift ones train the strength and perseverance of their pursuers.

Greenland seal hunter, *c.* 1830.

The fish and seals, on the other hand,

> have been cast aside into the godless and titanic region, as into a Limbo of the Unblessed, where the rational and intelligent part of the soul has been extinguished. Having, however, only a last remnant of sensation that is clogged with mud and deluged with water, they seem to be at their last gasp rather than alive.[4]

There was 'no glory in fishing', and thus little sport in seal-hunting. Seals were netted both on land and in the water, or clubbed and speared. In classical times, being so flabby, they were difficult to kill unless struck on the temple, or the head cut off. The flesh was not greatly esteemed, except by those with no alternative. Galen, the Greek physician, considered it distasteful and slimy, not palatable except by common people, and only then with mustard and vinegar sauce.[5] In a late fourth- or early fifth-century compilation of recipes attributed to Apicius, the Roman epicure, there is no mention of seal meat at all (although the author mentions everything else).

Seals were also traditionally hunted with nets and clubs in the northern islands, and here too there was some reluctance to eat seal, the inhabitants complaining that 'there was a terrible smell off the flesh'.[6] Despite this unsavoury assessment, people on the island of Uist, Shetland (home of the MacCodrum clan), would salt the flesh of seals and 'in the time of Lent eat them as sweetly as venison', treating them as fish rather than flesh. In North Ronaldsha (now Ronaldsay) seals were captured for eating, and 'were said to make good hams'.[7] The hunters who pursued the elephant seals on the remote islands of the southern seas were forced to live off seal meat for months at a time. The 'beef' was not relished, being 'black, oily, and indigestible', but the sealers did eat the tongue, as well as the heart and the trunks, the latter served stuffed and roasted and known to devotees as 'snotters'.[8] Seal liver was also savoured by sailors and sealers, but too much was not a good thing. The Spanish and Portuguese who sealed the coasts of Africa (naming capes and islands 'Lobo' after the sea-wolves they hunted) complained of suffering from consuming too much seal. Seal liver concentrates vitamin A, particularly in the bearded seal, and there are reports of illness connecting over-consumption and hypervitaminosis, which results in drowsiness, headaches, vomiting and peeling of the skin.[9]

Flippers are also choice cuts, which continue to be enjoyed among seal hunting cultures. While the ringed seal is most often hunted for food, the bearded seal furnishes a particular delicacy for the Inupiat in Alaska – fermented flippers. 'Fermenting' meat by caching it in excavations in the permafrost is a traditional method of preserving flesh and achieving a desired potent flavour.[10] Newfoundlanders, too, have always enjoyed a feed of fresh seal in the spring, and flippers are traditionally baked into a pie, sometimes with the 'fingers' poking up through the crust.[11]

Flesh was not, however, the object of the traditional European seal hunt. It was the skin that was desirable, being tough and waterproof. The hides made excellent and long-wearing shoe leather, though many complained of the rank, briny odour. (In Orkney, it was said that the boots wore well as long as you did not walk in them below the mark of the high tide, when they would exhibit their affinity to the sea.)[12] In Europe, the skins of young harp seals were 'manufactured into hose, for they are very tenacious, and when properly prepared, they keep out wet better even than prepared calf-skin'. Sealskin sandals or sealskin inserts were also recommended as a remedy for those afflicted with gout.[13] In the sixteenth century, Konrad Gesner noted that he had 'heard of belts being made of the skin of a seal for the

wearing of swords, three fingers in width and hairy'. These were completely black, 'soft and smooth like a silken fleece shining from afar' and highly valued.[14]

The value of the seal's hide may also have had something to do with the more magical properties attributed to it. Because the seal was never struck by lightning, the skin was proof against that peril (though the virgin Thecla called the wrath of god down on the monster seals in the form of a lightning bolt). Caesar Augustus wore an amulet of sealskin for protection, while Pliny suggested that a tent of seal-hide would protect its inhabitants from a thunderbolt. Farmers would drag a piece of sealskin around their fields to ward off hailstorms, and sailors would nail a fragment to the mast to protect against wind and storm. Eminent naturalists such as Pliny and Gesner reported that sailors wore belts of sealskin that bristled according to bad weather or changing tides, the skin showing a lingering sympathy with the sea.[15] These attributes might account for the fact that in fourth-century Rome an untanned seal hide was worth more than a leopard or lion skin.[16] Seal flippers, those curious appendages,

Sebastiano del Piombo, *Anton Francesco degli Albizzi,* wearing sealskin, 1525.

also had an unusual use for insomniacs. Pliny averred that 'No animal has a deeper sleep than this', and that the right fin has 'a certain soporiferous influence . . . that, if placed under the head, it induces sleep'.[17] Seals hauled out on land or coastal rocks were notoriously sleepy, and Buffon remarked with some exasperation on a monk seal that slept frequently during the day, snoring so loud that it was heard at a considerable distance. When asleep it could be roused only with difficulty; and when drowsy, would not promptly attend to his master.

Baron Cuvier also noted that the seals in the Paris Ménagerie had 'a great tendency to repose; sleep throughout the live-long night, and during the day cannot be kept awake without unceasing perseverance'.[18] This indolence, observed both in the wild and in captivity, did not enhance the seal's reputation, particularly among the fishers, who saw their nets torn and catch ravened by seals too lazy to fish for themselves. A salmon fisher of Nairn complained:

They live like toffs . . . Nothing is too good for them, only the tenderest part of the flesh. And often times they kill for the sake of killing – like a cat with mice. And one of

A very sleepy Hawaiian monk seal at French Frigate Shoals, Hawaii.

them will do a hundred pounds of damage to the nets in a night.[19]

No wonder then that old seal hunters in the northern islands wore a purse 'made from the skin of the paw of a seal' for luck.[20] The life of the seal seemed very fortunate.

If sealskin was lucky, other seal products were considered miracle remedies. The thick blubber was part of the classical pharmacopeia, used for everything from a cure for baldness in men to treatment of mange in horses. Seal fat was rubbed on boils and sores and was recommended in the treatment of rabies, which also included wrapping the patient in a sealskin. Melted seal fat was inserted in the nostrils of a woman suffering from 'hysterical suffocation', or obstructed respiration, attributed to the wandering of the uterus about the body. An unpleasant substance – and what could smell worse than seal? – would drive the womb back down into its proper place. Garlic and seal oil were also combined in a fumigant to open the cervix.[21] More

A grey seal eating fish.

116

prosaically, seal fat was used to cure leather. Another sovereign remedy involved the 'rennet' of the seal. Rennet is usually derived from the inner lining of a cow's many-chambered stomach. Since seals were like marine cows, it was assumed that they must also have rennet – anatomically impossible – and this was useful in treating female hysteria, quinsy, tetanus and, especially, epilepsy. (The 'rennet' was likely to be the curdled milk found inside the stomach of a young seal, often vomited up on capture.) The Roman writer Aelian accused the seal of being a 'malignant creature', since a seal will 'vomit up the curdled milk from its stomach so that epileptics may not be cured thereby'.[22] Ah, the perfidy of seals.

Even in the sixteenth century, European doctors were recommending seal meat, despite its noxious taste, as well as dried seal blood dissolved in wine, and the livers, lungs, spleens and stomachs of young seals were thought to cure 'epilepsy, giddiness, strokes, frenzy and other illnesses of the brain'. Some of the prescriptions for seal parts seem more magical than medicinal:

The right eye put into the skin of a deer will make one loveable, fortunate and powerful. Similarly the bearing of its heart and rennet averts every difficulty and brings every good. If also you were to carry its whiskers, I emphasise large and sharp ones, wrapped in the skin of a deer, and were to fall into the company of enemies, all would greet you as friends. Its tongue worn beneath your shoes brings victory. If anyone takes the heart of a seal, the tip of its tongue, the whiskers of its nose, either eye and its rennet and binds these things into the skin of a deer or of a seal and then wears it, he will vanquish everyone on land and sea.[23]

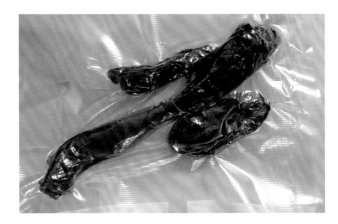

'Canada Seal Penis, Big', available for sale online.

Lest it be assumed that the belief in the potent power of seal parts is a thing of the past, in 1998 the Newfoundland sealer Michael Dwyer recounted his experience in shipping seal penises to China, where they have a role in traditional Chinese medicine:

> An old dog organ, as every sealer knows, brings in the best kind of money. Last year, on our first trip, we had brought in 550, almost a large fish containerful. Very discreetly, they were loaded onto a pickup that disappeared in the night. We received more money from that tub of organs than we did from the tractor-trailer loaded with pelt, meat and fat. Asians loved them. Nothing less than six inches was acceptable. They averaged seventy dollars each and we only had to handle them twice.[24]

OIL FROM ELEPHANTS

Oil rendered from seal fat was a traditional fuel among seal hunting peoples. It filled the soapstone *kudlik* or *quilliq* (oil-lamps) used by Inuit throughout the Arctic, and was also a valued commodity in Europe. As early as the mid-fifteenth century, Portuguese and Spanish sealers established processing stations for seal oil on islands and sandbanks along the Gold and Ivory Coasts, rendering the fat and returning to Europe with loads of skins and barrels of oil. It was, however, the discovery of the elephants of the sea that made seal oil an end in itself. The remote colonies of the sea elephants were first discovered by Europeans in the mid-eighteenth century, and the sailors found

> no difficulty in killing them, since they were incapable of either resisting or escaping, their motion being more unwieldy than can be conceived: their blubber, all the time they are moving, is agitated in large waves under the skin.

There was often a foot of fat beneath the skin, and the largest male 'frequently yielded a butt of oil'. The oil served the sealers for 'burning in lamps, or mixing with pitch to pay the ship's sides, or, when worked up with wood-ashes, to supply the use of tallo[w]'.[25] Seal oil, like whale oil, was the petroleum of its day, and by the 1820s the profit from the sale of barrels of the

Kudlik, a soapstone oil-lamp, from the Coppermine River, c. 1903.

Sea-elephant Fishery, drawing by H. W. Elliott after Captain H. C. Chester, 19th century.

clean-burning oil in London, Madrid or New York made up for the long voyages and horrendous conditions of the hunt.[26] And the conditions were horrific, for both beast and man. The casual brutality of the elephant seal harvest was surprising even by nineteenth-century standards. Robert Hamilton, writing less than a century after the European discovery of the great beasts, described how the elephants were traditionally killed by the 'most formidable of their enemies', the natives of New Holland and Van Dieman's Land (Australia and Tasmania, respectively):

> The moment that the native savages perceive one they surround it, while it in vain attempts to regain the sea. Its retreat thus cut off, armed with long pieces of wood burning at one end, the savages attack the unfortunate brute. As soon as he opens his mouth, showing the only weapons with which he is armed, they all at once force many of these flaming torches down his throat. The unfortunate Elephant gives utterance to the most melancholy bellowings, his whole frame is agitated with violence, and he dies of suffocation and agony.

But this woeful practice was as nothing compared to the depredations of the European fleets. On the seals' remote island fastnesses, there is, in Hamilton's words,

> no escape from mercantile cupidity, which appears to have vowed complete extinction to the race. The fishers use in destroying them a lance twelve or fifteen feet long, with a sharp iron point of about two feet. With great address, they seize the moment when the animal raises his left fore-paw to advance, and plunging the weapon to the heart, he immediately falls down drenched in blood. The females rarely offer the least opposition, their defensive weapons being feebler still than those of the male. When attacked, they seek to flee; if prevented they become violently agitated, their countenance assumes the expression of despair, and they weep piteously. 'I have myself,' says Peron [the French naturalist], 'seen a young female shed tears abundantly, whilst one of our wicked and cruel sailors amused himself at the sight, knocking out her teeth with an oar, whenever she opened her mouth. The poor animal might have softened a heart of stone; its mouth streaming with blood, and its eyes with tears.'[27]

The disregard of the 'elephanters' for the apparent humanity of the seal was reflected in the offhand comments of Rallier du Baty, an early twentieth-century French visitor to the Desolation Islands (so aptly named by Captain Cook, and now called Kerguelen Islands), who remarked that 'One need not sentimentalize over sea elephants. Their only use to the world is to provide blubber.' A former elephanter turned mammalogist and champion of the elephant seals, L. Harrison Matthews, objected to this cruel observation, noting that 'slaughtering seals always degrades and brutalizes those who do it.'[28]

The sealers themselves lived under appalling conditions. The elephanters were 'dropped off' in gangs on the rocky islands above Antarctica, and there they stayed sometimes for a year or more, living on seals, penguin eggs and 'wild cabbage', with salted meat, flour and molasses to supplement their diet. A contemporary visitor described their temporary accommodations – dark huts made of wild grass lined with sealskins, lit by lamps burning elephant oil. The sealers were scarcely describable. With 'their long beards, greasy seal-like habiliments, and grim, fiendlike complexions', they looked 'more like troops of demons from the infernal regions, than baptised Christian men, as they sallied forth with brandished clubs'.[29]

The great southern elephant seal herds that had greeted Joseph Banks and Captain Cook in the late eighteenth century ('the beach is encumber'd with their quantities') were long gone

Sealing in Antartica, an illustration from *The Cruise of the 'Antarctic' to the South Polar regions, etc*, by Henrik Johan Bull (1896).

122

by the time the southern seal oil industry dwindled at the end of the nineteenth century.[30] The historian Briton Cooper Busch calculated that more than one million of the southern species were killed during the course of the elephant oil rush. By the end of the century there was some protection for both elephants and fur seals (the other great southern harvest), and by 1933 Macquarie Island off Antarctica, the site of the last licensed hunt, was declared a sanctuary for birds and animals, and the seals began their slow recovery.

The northern elephant herds were less numerous than their southern cousins, and they had suffered even more from the oil rush. In the 1840s, the ship captain William Phelps, who had hunted the southern species, reported that the beaches at Santa Barbara Island off the coast of California were covered with seals, but just over a generation later few were to be found anywhere along the coast. In 1892 a Smithsonian expedition found only eight seals and shot seven for the museum's collection.[31] Oil from elephants had run dry.

'THE GREATEST HUNT IN THE WORLD'

Where the elephants lay in icy southern or temperate Pacific waters, high in the North Atlantic lived another source of oil, the herds of harp seals and their cousins, the hooded seals or 'hoods'. Each autumn, the harp seal population begins an annual migration from the polar regions, riding the Labrador Current, splitting at the straits of Belle Isle into two herds, one moving along the northern coast of Newfoundland, the other into the Gulf of St Lawrence. At the height of the annual migration, nine-teenth-century observers reported, 'the sea seems paved with their heads.'[32] For millennia, the human inhabitants of these regions had waited for the annual bounty of the seals, who as

surely as swallows followed their well-worn routes in the sea. The Dorset Eskimo hunters harpooned them as they swam by the shores of Newfoundland, and centuries later along the coasts of Labrador, European settlers would string coarse nets in the 'tickles' or narrow gaps between islands, or place fixed nets in 'seal frames' along the shores to catch the harps as they dove for fish. This winter seal hunt took the adult harps on their way south, but the great hunt targeted their pups as they returned north with the ice in the spring.

Unlike the elephant or the fur seals, the harp and hood seals spend their lives at sea. Each spring, millions of these ice-lovers haul out not on rocks or beaches, but on the great sheets of the Atlantic pack ice to whelp and rear their young, before returning to the polar seas. In late February new ice forms in the Gulf and off Southern Labrador, thin enough that the seals can maintain their breathing holes, but thick enough to support their masses. The whelping takes place in late February and early March, and so regular is the date that the Newfoundlanders would refer to the end of February as the 'seals' birthday'.

There are records of seals netted in the winter hunt in the early eighteenth century off the Newfoundland coasts, but the spring hunt, which has continued with such notoriety to the present day, commenced officially in 1793 when one boat returned with a 'bumper crop' of 800 seals. By the 1830s, half the adult male population of Newfoundland was engaged in what they called the 'seal fishery'. Like the elephant seal hunt, this seal harvest bore fruit in the form of hides and oil, the latter part of a global oil industry that began long before the first gusher blew in Texas. By the mid-eighteenth century, Europeans were using oil to light city streets, cure leather, lubricate machinery and make soap.

James Vey, seal processing in St John's, Newfoundland, late 19th or early 20th century.

Some of it came from plants – rapeseed and olive oil – but the best was 'train' oil from the whales and seals. 'Train' comes from the Dutch word *tran* or drop oil, so called because the oil drips from the fat without intervention. Pale seal oil was 'cold drawn' and burned clear and odourless, but profit demanded that as much oil as possible be rendered from the fat, and the brown seal oil resulting from pressing and boiling was very odiferous indeed. Making seal oil was, as a nineteenth-century Newfoundland writer observed, an exceedingly disagreeable operation 'from first to last, on account of the stench that accompanies it, and it makes St John's during July, August, and September, a most undesirable residence'.[33]

In the 1870s mineral oils derived from petroleum largely replaced seal oil as lubricants and lighting fuel, though the lighthouses of Newfoundland burned seal oil until the 1880s. While the oil trade had declined drastically in importance by the end of the nineteenth century, sealers continued to speak about getting 'into the fat', in homage to the original goal of the hunt. Stripped of their fat, sealskins were also part of the great global trade in leather, the precursor to oil-based plastics. Seal leather was used for boots and shoes, travelling trunks, waterproof breeches, gloves, belts, wallets and saddle covers. Sometimes elegant ladies sported sealskin muffs, and gentlemen 'waistcoats in the Greenland style'. The 'hair' sealskins were also an economical substitute for the more desirable fur seal pelts used to make highly fashionable Victorian ladies' coats – 'sealskin sacques' – but by the end of the nineteenth century, even these were replaced by a cheaper alternative:

> The skin substituted for the costly skin garments affected by wealthy ladies is a monkey skin got in west Africa, and seal sacques and caps are now so cheap, in consequence,

that they have ceased to be a badge of fashion and the wealthy will no longer wear them.[34]

By 1898 the price of skins was so low 'as to leave little or no profit', and seal products accounted for only 5 per cent of Newfoundland's exports, falling from a high of 30 per cent in the mid-century. But even if the markets were poor, men still clamoured to go to the seal fishery each spring. It filled the empty months till the cod returned, and it was a chance for many who lived on the 'tuck' system, owing their all to the merchants, to earn the only real cash income they saw in a year.[35] Beckles

Benjamin W. Hawkins, 'The Seal and the Walrus', lithograph, from *Graphic Illustrations of Animals shewing their utility to man . . .*, mid-19th century.

Seal fur coats for 'automobilistes', from Atelier Bachwitz, *Grand Album de Fourrures* (1908–10).

Wilson, a journalist from Montreal, understood the sealers' motivations:

> Some of them, the young especially, like the excitement and adventure of the hunt with all its hardships, for if they return successful they are the heroes of the hour; but with the great bulk it is 'their poverty, not their will,' that forces them on board. There are empty cupboards and hungry mouths at home, and the hope of returning with 'a good bill' makes them submit to any conditions.[36]

And the conditions were very poor. Like the elephanters on the desolate rocks of the Southern Ocean, the Newfoundland sealers endured an unbelievably brutal and brutalizing life. They converged on St John's from the outports, often walking for days through the snow, to vie for a coveted berth:

> It 'ud make your heart sore to see the way lots o' these islanders come aboard the sealin' vessels in the spring – wi' pinched half-starved faces, and hardly 'nough clothes to stand a summer breeze.[37]

Once on the ship, things rapidly got worse, as George Allan England discovered. An American writer of speculative fiction, in 1923 he begged a berth on the *Terra Nova*, a famous sealing steamer, to join the men he would call 'Vikings of the Ice' on 'the greatest hunt in the world'.[38] The *Terra Nova* was captained by the celebrated sealing captain Abraham Kean, the 'admiral of the Fleet', a man with a sure sense of how to sail his ship 'into the fat'. England was more than shocked by what he found:

Herbert G. Ponting, '*Terra Nova*, 1911', on the Scott Antarctic Expedition. The *Terra Nova* continued her career as a Newfoundland sealing vessel; she was estimated to have contained over 800,000 seal pelts during her years at the Front.

Poverty! Lord, what poverty! All was rough, dark, dirty – incredibly dirty, gorgeously and grotesquely dirty. And this at the beginning of the trip. Later, when the men had really 'grased deyselfs to de helbows in de fat,' and when everything had become tainted with grease and blood, and the sculps were stowed at the aft end of the 'tweendecks and many others were dragged through it to be flung below, forward, conditions there beggared description.

The sealers brought only one set of clothes, for most of them 'never wash or shave on the sealing racket'. According to the captains, the men were truly like brutes: 'Dirt doesn't hurt them and neither does hardship. Why, they're half seals themselves!'[39]

By the time England took his berth in the filthy cabin of the *Terra Nova*, the traditional seal hunt had morphed into something else. England called it a 'gorgeous epic of violence, hardship, and bloodshed'. Going to the ice had achieved an almost mythic status for Newfoundlanders and become a test of manhood, a rite of passage for green boys from the outports, and a time of camaraderie for the veterans of the hunt. Theirs was the only sealing fleet in the world, commanded by men who were national heroes and masters of the ice. It was the Newfoundland sealing captain Bob Bartlett who guided the American explorer Robert Peary on his attempts to reach the pole. No wonder England wanted to take part in the epic voyage of the sealers under the legendary 'Cap'n Kean', one of 'the genuine old heart of oak breed of mariners, now, alas, dying out'.[40] The Newfoundlanders made up songs about the exploits of hardy crews, gallant captains and their steel ships. These verses were published in a St John's newspaper on the eve of the First World War:

Come all you jolly Northern men, and hear me while I sing
Of skippers and of ships, all going to the ice this spring;
There's Bowring's fleet, that can't be beat by any on our
  shore,
In their *Steph-a-no*, A. Kean will go, our handy
  Commodore.
Their *Florizel*, I beg to tell, will take out his son Joe,
With Kenneth Knee, the *Ranger* she, will range the icy
  floe.
. . .
Bob Bartlett, in the *Neptune*, goes to try his luck once
  more,
'Twas he who guided Peary when the Pole he did
  explore;
. . .
The names of captains and of ships now to you I did tell,
And I pray that every one of them this spring may pan
  out well;
And may kind Heaven waft them with a sweet and
  pleasant gale,
Unto success, may Fortune Bless, our noble nineteen
  sail,
To mothers and wives, God save the lives, of those who
  sail these ships,
And send them home, across the foam, to us with
  bumper trips.[41]

But fortune did not always bless the fleet, and year after year
ships were crushed in the ice, holed and sunk. The seal pelts would
run and the oil catch fire. Men were infected with 'sealfinger' (a
severe form of cellulitis), or suffered frostbite, snow blindness,
pneumonia or nasty wounds from gaffs or knives, or even from

the teeth of an old 'dog hood'. The sealers were nevertheless notoriously hardy, seemingly indifferent to the hardships and peril of their work. Beckles Wilson observed them working in their shirtsleeves in sub-zero temperatures and 'as oblivious to the dangers of drowning or being crushed to death by ice as one of the seals themselves'.[42] There were tragedies, however, that stunned even the fearless Newfoundlanders and shook the island. It was the famous Abraham Kean who was blamed by many for the great sealing disaster of 1914, when 78 sealers from the *Newfoundland*, captained by his son Wes, died, stranded on the ice in a blizzard for two days:

> Men were discovered huddled in groups, frozen solidly together as if they had tried in vain to warm each other, all shrouded under the same palls of snow that inwrapped the dead seals, victims of their fruitless butchery . . . One father and his son were brought in, the stiffened arms of the father still clinging to his boy, trying to the very end

to shield him. They had to be winched up . . . fast-frozen together.[43]

Despite the peril, Newfoundlanders continued to go to the ice. Like the seal hunters of the Mediterranean and the Northern Isles (some of whom might also claim to be 'half seal'), the New-foundland fishers looked on the hunt as a welcome part of the annual cycle of subsistence, a godsend in the cold winter months before cod fishing resumed in the spring. They classified seals as fish and the Church gave them special dispensation to eat them on Fridays and during Lent. If the seals were not exactly fish, then they were like oceanic sheep, found 'sleeping in what are called seal meadows of the ice', where they 'were attacked with fire-arms or bludgeons, and slaughtered in great numbers'.[44] The seal hunt permeated the entire culture, with its vocabulary of ice – pans, slob, knots and pinnacles – and of seal: swile, whitecoat, bedlamer (from the French *bête de la mer*), blueback, dog hood, sculp, scutters and flippers. The lives of the inhabitants of the northern bays of Newfoundland were as much shaped by seals as the lives of the seals were by the greatest hunt.

'PEOPLE OF THE PLACE WHERE THERE IS SEAL'

While Newfoundlanders might eat and occasionally wear seal, to the inhabitants of Greenland and the Canadian Arctic, the seal was more than just an incidental item of diet. David Crantz was sent to Greenland in 1759 by the Moravian Church, and soon realized that for the native inhabitants seals were the staff of life and the basis of the economy:

Seals are more needful to them than sheep are to us, though they supply us with food and raiment, or than the

cocoa-tree to the Indian, although it presents him with meat and clothing, houses, and ships; so that in case of necessity they could live upon them alone. The Seal's flesh supplies them with palatable and substantial food; the fat is sauce to their other aliment, and furnishes them with oil for light and fire, while at the same time it contributes to their wealth in every form, seeing that they barter it for all kinds of ne-cessaries. They sew better with the fibres of Seal's sinews than with thread or silk; of the fine internal membranes they make their body raiment, and their windows; of the skins they make their buoys, so much used in fishing, and many domestic utensils, and, of the coarser kinds, their tents, and their boats of all sizes, in which they voyage and seek provisions; therefore, no man can pass for a right Greenlander who cannot catch Seals.[45]

Sealskin boot, from Disko Island, Greenland, 1934.

Hans Egede, an eighteenth-century Norwegian missionary who translated the Lord's Prayer into the language of the Greenland Eskimo, could find no better word to convey the sense of 'daily bread' than seal, and so congregations were taught to pray, 'Give us this day our seal.'[46]

It is not only the Greenlanders who lived by the seal. The Netsilik Inuit, who live in the northern reaches of Nunavut in Arctic Canada, are defined by their name, 'People of the place where there is seal'. When the Arctic explorer Knud Rasmussen, himself a child of Greenland, went on a seal hunt with the Netsilik hunter Inugtuk in 1923, they began with a jug of boiling seal's blood, the stirrup cup of the Arctic. Rasmussen followed the hunters as they sought out the breathing holes of the ringed seal, where they crouched for hours in the freezing Arctic winds waiting for the telltale sign that a seal was rising to breathe. Then they would strike with their toggle harpoon, and if they were lucky,

(top left) John White, *Kalicho, an Inuk from Frobisher Bay*; wearing sealskin suit, 1585–93, watercolour.

John White, *Arnaq and Nutaaq, Inuit from Frobisher Bay*, 1585–93, watercolour.

Greenland Eskimo, with clothing and equipment, 1880, lithograph.

Seal hunting
in Greenland,
illustration from
Hans Egede,
*Description et
histoire naturelle
du Groenland*
(1763).

haul in a seal. On the day Rasmussen hunted, fifteen hunters
went out for eleven hours, and brought back one seal. Still they
were thankful for Sedna's gift, and they shared a 'hunter's meal',
described as:

> a regular procedure almost in the nature of a sacrament
> ... The liver and blubber are ... cut up into dice and eaten

Inuit hunters dragging seals on spring snow, early 20th century.

Inuit skinning a seal.

kneeling. For myself, I always felt there was something touching and solemn about this ceremonial eating of the first meat on which men's lives depend.[47]

In 1968 the National Film Board of Canada and the Educational Development Center in the u.s. sought to document a way of life they felt was fast disappearing. They asked the Inuit at Pelly

Bay in Canada's Northwest Territories, they who called themselves the people of the seal, to re-enact the old ways, including a seal hunt on the spring ice. The remarkable series of short films that resulted has been used as sometimes controversial teaching material in North American schools and they are now readily available on the internet. They are breathtaking. In the two-part film 'At the Spring Ice', the film-makers follow an Inuit family on their daily round. The father hunts the seal by stealth and skill. He sets out across the ice armed with a toggle harpoon crafted

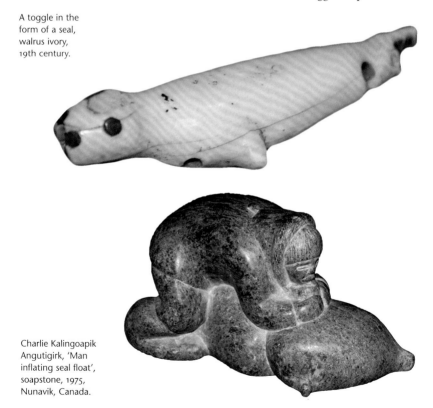

A toggle in the form of a seal, walrus ivory, 19th century.

Charlie Kalingoapik Angutigirk, 'Man inflating seal float', soapstone, 1975, Nunavik, Canada.

A hunter in Greenland with rifle and traditional hunting sail, 1999.

from bone, and pieces of caribou skin. As he nears the seal's place, he falls to the ground. Lying down, he transforms into a seal, wriggling forward on the skins, waving his feet and hand in the air like flippers, scratching the snow with a claw of caribou antler, and grunting and calling in the ancient language of seal. The seal raises his head – ah, just another seal like myself, resting on the ice. Closer and closer the hunter comes until he rises, the seal sees his enemy, and plunges into his breathing hole. The hunter aims, and misses. The seal slides away beneath the ice. Finally, days later, the hunter takes a seal, and the animal, transformed from lithe beast to flabby furred slug, is dragged back to camp. Here the hunter's wife transforms pelt to skin, strips of skin to thongs, and flesh to food for humans and dogs. Sealskin becomes boots

Ribs from a young harp seal (*Phoca groenlandica*), bought in Upernavik, Greenland.

and bags.[48] In addition to the small ringed seal, both bearded and hooded seals furnish the base materials for much of Inuit material culture. Bearded and hood sealskin is used for skin boats, house coverings and women's clothing, the stomachs converted into traditional inflatable fishing buoys.

More than 70 years after Rasmussen hunted seals with the Netsilik, the American hunter Ted Kerasote went after seals in Greenland with Lars Olsen, a master of hunting the basking seals – *uuttoq* – with a shooting sled and sail.[49] The Netsilik sliding skins had been replaced by a sled, the harpoon by a rifle, and the man was disguised not by his gestures, but hidden behind a white shooting sail.[50] Ted and Lars caught and ate a seal, the liver raw, the heart boiled ('salty, and delicious'), the cooked ribs tasting 'like mutton gone to sea – thick, greasy, and with a hint of kelp', and the boiled intestine, 'like squid dipped in wasabi sauce'.[51] To the Inuit and the Greenlanders the seal is table meat, taken with considerable effort, traditional and healthy food from the land. It is also highly symbolic and representative of traditional ways. When in 2009 Michaëlle Jean, the Governor General and the Queen's Representative in Canada, shared a feast of raw seal meat during an official visit to Nunavut in the Canadian Arctic, she set off a firestorm of controversy concerning the morality of eating seal. Animal rights activists and vegetarians decried her actions, calling her a 'Neanderthal', but Jean was unapologetic, as were the Inuit.[52] For them the ringed seal hunt

Alungelah, a Kenepetoo Inuit Chief, Fullerton, Hudson Bay, wearing sealskin clothing. From Geraldine Moodie album, 1903.

should be no more distressing than the deer or rabbit hunt of the south. The celebrated Inuit throat-singer Tanya Tagaq attempted in her 2009 short film, *Tungijuq* (What We Eat), to convey something of the viewpoint of the people of the seal. *Tungijuq* is a visceral and hauntingly beautiful essay on the hunt, the Inuit and transformation, a cinematic riposte to those whose harvest has never been from the sea.[53] That harvest is now endangered by the protest against the Newfoundland seal hunt, which has decimated the market for seal products in North America and Europe and turned the Inuit, the Greenlanders and the Newfoundlanders into defenders of the hunt.

5 Whitecoat

They are, in general, patient and submissive creatures, and harmless to man, to whose power and love of gain doubtless not less than a million to a million and a half fall victims each year.[1]

Joel Asaph Allen, 1880

By the time Allen lamented the victims of greed, the nineteenth-century seal hunt in the northern oceans was in decline, seal oil no longer being necessary to light the streets of London. Numbers such as Allen cited were never seen again, as the fleets shrank and the price of oil and skins fell. There was some revival during the First World War in the Newfoundland seal hunt, but the ships were few and the catch on average less than half of the boom years. More significantly, the size of the herds also dwindled, particularly off the Norwegian island of Jan Mayen and in the White Sea where they were hunted. Norway has always been a sealing nation, and as the seal population off their own shores showed the effects of big harvests in the 1920s and '30s, they began to eye the other side of the Atlantic. The first Norwegian ship hunted hoods in Newfoundland waters in 1937, and after their steel ice-breakers were banned by the Russians from the White Sea in 1946, they sailed for the Front, what seal hunters call the ice sheets off Newfoundland where the seals gather. By 1971 the Newfoundland hunt was effectively in Norwegian hands, though the ships sailed from Halifax, and the pelts were processed in Trinity Bay.

The Canadian seal hunt became the last of the great commercial marine mammal hunts. The oil rush for the elephants of the sea was long over; the fashion for the sealskin sacque made from the pelts of fur seals had had its day; and the walrus was protected

Theodore de Bry's map of Novaya Zemlya and the White Sea, drawn by Gerhardo de Veer, 1601, showing walruses and seals.

from the ivory poacher. The harp seal hunt, and to a lesser extent the hood seal hunt, continued, not only at the Front and in the Gulf of St Lawrence but in the sea off Greenland and Norway and in the White Sea, though the numbers taken in European and Russian waters were dwarfed by the scale of the Canadian 'harvest'.

Seal oil was no longer the principal target of the hunt. Now it was the fur trade that drove the sealing industry. The fashion for sealskin in Europe and North America demanded the pelts not only of the young of the harp seal – the whitecoats – but those of the 'bluebacks', or young hoods, to be transformed into luxury apparel, which unlike seal leather used for belts and shoes was instantly recognizable as sealskin.[2] Seal became so desirable that fake seal coats were marketed to the young and impecunious in Canada. (I know, because I wore one.) The fake fur resembled the silvery spotted skin of the juvenile harp, but felt like polyester. It was, however, the height of fashion. Prices for skins meant more demand on the herds, and between 1949 and 1961 an average of 300,000 seals, mostly pups, were taken annually by the sealing fleets and the landsmen who hunted in smaller vessels from the shores of Newfoundland and Quebec. Scientists in Canada began to question the sustainability of the herds but unless the sealers operated within the three-mile limit (the 200-mile limit was only declared in 1977), there was little regulation possible. In 1963 Canada moved the closing date of the hunt to 30 April from 5 May (24 April in the Gulf), and in 1964 a limit of 50,000 young harps was set for the Gulf. But it was too late.

The Îles de la Madeleine (the Magdalens) are islands in the Gulf of St Lawrence, a part of Quebec, with a traditional economy that was based on fishing and, in the spring, sealing. In 1964 Artek Films arrived on the islands to make a documentary on the hardy Madelinots, and their annual harvest of the ice. This was a period when Quebec, the distinct French-speaking province of Canada, was celebrating its particular heritage, and documenting traditional hunting and fishing practices, including that of the seal hunters. What Artek filmed (*Les Grands Phoques de la banquise*) shocked audiences in Montreal and Quebec City, and later outraged the Germans, who were among the biggest consumers of seal products.[3] The film showed the hunters clubbing young seals, then skinning them, and in one famous sequence a young seal moves and screams after skinning. Government officials accused the film-makers of staging the atrocity, but the seal was out of the bag, and would not be put back.

Protests against hunting seals did not begin with the 1960s, the decade of protests for many causes. There have always been humans who love seals. The great grey seals – the selkies – were the first mammal protected by British Parliament in 1914. And just as the awkward, ugly sea elephants found their devotees in the nineteenth century, so did the harp seals of Newfoundland. Philip Tocque, a Newfoundlander, went to the ice in 1834, and never forgot his early experience:

> The seal fishery is a constant scene of bloodshed and slaughter. Here you behold a heap of seals writhing and crimsoning the ice with their blood, rolling from side to side in dying agony. There you see another lot, while the last spark of life is not yet extinguished, being stripped of their skins and fat, their writhings and heavings making the unpractised hand shrink with horror to touch them.[4]

The Montreal-born journalist Beckles Wilson, while mostly sympathetic to Newfoundland and its difficult situation at the end of the nineteenth century, was appalled by the seal hunt:

> I say that the annual seal hunt of Newfoundland is one great carnival of cruelty and bloodshed, I say that which not every witness to, but every participant in, its horrors readily admits . . . The destruction begins quite without prelude. One or two blows on the head fractures the skull of the young seal, if the gaff be in the hands of an old sealer. Others of the group are treated in like fashion, to the chorus of heart-rending cries and sobs. Almost at the same moment the knife is brought into play, and the skin and fat detached from the carcases, which, still quivering with life 'often struggling, and occasionally still whimpering' are instantly surrounded by the miserable mother. Her moans, as it gazes upon the sickening, moving red masses, all that is left of her children, are fearful to hear.

It is now the rude details of the slaughterhouse over again. Clots of gore cover the hands and limbs, and even the faces, of the men; the ice is stained and slippery with mingled blood and fat; the air reeks with the smell of blood, and still that low human whimper goes up, and the slaughter goes on.[5]

There were two aspects of the hunt that combined to make it an object of revulsion for many observers – the first was the effect on the seals, and the second on the sealers. Adding fire to the fat was the charm of the baby-faced seal pup.

'MURDER IN THE NURSERY'

'There's no doubt in my mind that the baby harp seal is one of the loveliest creatures on earth.'[6] Brian Davies, who founded the International Fund for Animal Welfare (IFAW), one of the strongest voices against the annual harp seal hunt in Canada, saw his first whitecoat in March 1965. 'Walking carefully across some loose, broken ice, I came across my first baby harp seal. I was spellbound . . . By the end of that day I knew that I belonged to the seals.'[7] Davies is not the only observer to have been charmed by a 'bundle of white fluff'. George Allan England, at the Front off northeastern Newfoundland with the 'Vikings of the Ice' in 1924, was equally taken with the 'engaging infants':

The woolly little beggars look up at you with a couple of ravishing dark-brown eyes continually suffused with heart-melting tears, needing only a ribbon round their necks (if they have necks, which doesn't seem apparent) to fit them for prize winners in any beauty show.[8]

Paul Watson, a Greenpeace veteran and the controversial captain of the *Sea Shepherd*, while rescuing a 'little tyke' on the ice was 'touched by his incredible beauty and innocence'.[9] Robert Hunter, the co-founder of Greenpeace, felt that given the whitecoat's appearance, 'God loved it more than almost any other creature.'[10] It was not just the snow-white offspring of the harp seals that evoked this response. In January 1958 newspaper headlines in Britain screamed 'Murder in the Nursery', reflecting the controversy over a proposed grey seal cull: 'The friendly grey seals who sing happily on the Farne Islands are in trouble. Murder is planned in their nursery.'[11] These were more than young animals; they were the babies of the sea.

Harp seal mother and pup.

148

A young grey seal
in Helgoland,
North Sea.

'THE CRUEL HUNT'

Brian Davies went to the ice in the Gulf of St Lawrence in 1965 as an observer from the Canadian Society for the Prevention of Cruelty to Animals (SPCA). This was the first year that the Government of Canada, responding to criticism of the hunt and the public relations disaster of the Artek film, had imposed a quota on the number of whitecoats killed in the Gulf. Fisheries officers were dispatched to ensure the quota was not exceeded, and Humane Society representatives were sent to respond to the accusations of cruelty. Davies and his colleague were not allowed to view the actual killing of the pups, but they saw the evidence of the hunt left behind on the ice:

> The once virgin ice was splattered with blood. The freshly skinned carcasses of seal pups lay silent as the steam from their skinless bodies rose in the chill air. Even the water flowed red.[12]

Seal hunting was inherently a bloody business. George Allan England, on board the *Terra Nova*, was astounded by the quantities of gore – 'Niagaras of blood cascade. A seal appears to be merely a bag of blood and fat.'[13] But while the quantities might have been disturbing, particularly against the background of what one observer called the 'thousand cathedral-like spires and pinnacles' of the white ice, accusations of both waste and cruelty provoked the most criticism.[14] There is little meat on a very young seal, and though some meat from older seals (notably flippers) had always been eaten by sealers and their families, for the most part the skinned carcass was discarded on the ice. Though he admired the 'perfect' technique of the ice-hunters, England was nevertheless angered by what he called 'a wanton waste of life and of commercial values. In this hungry world, the sheer flinging away of these immense masses of edible meat is downright criminal.' It was not only the steaming carcasses staining the ice; there was something disturbing about the whitecoat pelts:

> In came the sculps, fur side to the ice, flesh side quivering like currant jelly – quivering and smoking. The thin streams of life departing, not yet quite gone, hung tenuously. And on those sculps the flippers wagged and waved like little hands, bidding farewell for ever to the world of ice.[15]

Seals are hard to kill, or as Robert Hamilton put it, 'tenacious of life'. Writing in 1839, when a new consciousness on the humane treatment of animals had only begun to stir in Britain, Hamilton was shocked by the abuses of the seal hunt:

> many cruelties have been perpetrated upon them, which most who have witnessed declare to be too horrible for description, and over which we willingly draw a veil. If life

is to be sacrificed, there is a right way of taking it as well as a wrong, and we insist that the former should be followed, and the latter avoided.[16]

Hamilton's sentiments were echoed over a century later in 1955, when two British observers toured humane societies in North America, condemning the seal hunt as 'degrading and cruel'. They also spoke out against waste, observing seals shot and sinking, or wounded and escaping to die in open water.[17] A decade later, Brian Davies was shocked by the 'open air abattoir' and by what he witnessed not only in the skinning of whitecoats, but in the shooting and clubbing of adult seals:

> It is a day I would rather forget – except for the fact that the remembrance of that day and all other days at the killing grounds in subsequent years only served to fuel my belief that the cruel hunt must be stopped . . . We saw so many sights, so many horrors, on that first day of the hunt. It was not a place for the squeamish and time and again I felt the bile rising in my throat as we stumbled across some new facet of this savage trade.[18]

Davies was convinced there was no way to regulate the hunt properly, given the vastness of the ice, the small number of officials and the very nature of the hunt itself, 'inherently inhumane'.[19] For the next decade, he devoted his considerable talents to ending the hunt. He soon learned the power of popular media when in 1966 he persuaded a journalist for *Weekend Magazine*, a pictorial distributed weekly with Canadian newspapers coast to coast, to write about 'The Cruel Seal Hunt'. In the following years, stories appeared in the London *Daily Mirror* ('The Price of a Sealskin Coat'), *Paris Match* and other foreign press, aimed at the consumer end of the chain – the fashionable men and women who sported sealskin coats. In 1969 Davies left the Humane Society to found IFAW, 'to stop this cruel hunt for seals'. Despite his success in branding the seal hunt as inhumane, by 1976 Davies could not yet declare victory against the sealing industry. That spring, he went to the ice not only with Silver Donald Cameron, another writer for *Weekend Magazine*, and dozens of reporters and photographers, but with four airline stewardesses, whose presence would be sure to draw media attention. Like others before them, they were horrified by the scenes of bloodshed. Cameron wrote in his article, 'What we're watching is comparable to killing kittens with claw hammers.'[20]

THE 'THREE-RING CIRCUS'[21]

If it was Davies who first brought the charges of cruelty to a wider world through his 'Save the Seals' campaign and IFAW, it was Greenpeace that made the whitecoat a global symbol for eco-warriors and environmental crusaders. In 1976 Paul Watson, then a member of Greenpeace in Vancouver, placed an advertisement in an alternative weekly, the *Georgia Straight*, that with counter-culture aplomb echoed the text of Ernest Shackleton's famed recruitment poster for his Antarctic expedition:

> WANTED
>
> Twelve crew members needed for hazardous environmental protest expedition. No wages, bitter cold, three weeks of constant danger living upon the moving ice fields of the Labrador Front. The Task: To shepherd the baby harp seals and protect them from the brutal clubs of the Canadian and Norwegian sealers. The reward: the saving of a species from biological extinction.

152

While not exactly living on the ice (the group stayed in a 'cozy family boarding house' in St Anthony and helicoptered to the Front), the members did adopt a new form of protest, saving one seal at a time by covering the pups with their bodies or scooping them to safety. As Watson put it, when he left his rescued pup to return to the helicopters, 'Things got kind of personal at that point. He was no longer any seal. I knew him now and he knew me. We were buddies who had met on a battlefield.'[22]

Watson and Greenpeace brought new rhetoric and new tactics to the anti-seal hunt campaign. Watson saw himself as an eco-warrior and his team as 'a handsome collection of young eco-hawks'. When Watson and Hunter placed themselves between a seal and an icebreaker, they went up against the 'bloodthirsty Goliaths of Doom'.[23] The language of the battlefield began to dominate, and the 'seal meadows' became 'killing fields'. In 1977, based out of Blanc-Sablon on the Quebec north shore to avoid the 'occupied zone' around St Anthony where IFAW was quartered, Watson flew to the ice and confronted the sealers themselves. Reaching the *Martin Karlsen*, a Norwegian vessel, he handcuffed himself to the winch that was used to bring the seal pelts on board. Bruised, battered and ultimately rescued by the sealers, Watson returned to Blanc-Sablon to be greeted by the sealing protest's greatest weapon to date, Brigitte Bardot. As Greenpeace founder Robert Hunter said, 'Until her arrival the "seal hunt" story was all blood and death, but now it was blood and death and sex.'[24]

Bardot came to the hunt at the invitation of Franz Weber, a European environmentalist, who brought more than 70 European journalists to the ice. The photogenic Bardot, a cinema icon in her generation, was ferried to the ice in a Greenpeace helicopter, where she posed cheek-to-cheek with a young whitecoat.[25] The image appeared throughout Europe, and despite internal dissent in Greenpeace about such tactics, Bardot's star power did have an almost immediate effect. In 1977 the U.S. government passed a resolution condemning the Canadian hunt. More significantly, in 1982 the European Economic Community (EEC), responding to lobbying from IFAW as well as the publicity surrounding the hunt, voted to ban the import of baby harp and hood skins.

Yet the hunt continued, and in 1983 supporters of the ban launched another campaign. It was hard to resist the advertisements in *Le Monde* to 'SAUVEZ LES BÉBÉS PHOQUES' ('Save the baby seals'), with their photographs of big-eyed whitecoats, or the demands for immediate action: 'ARRETEZ LE MASSACRE: DANS QUELQUES JOURS 120,000 BÉBÉS PHOQUES VONT ETRE ASSASSINÉS ('Stop the massacre; in a few days 120,000 baby seals will be slaughtered'). If this was not enough to stop the hunt, IFAW also organized a postcard campaign to boycott Canadian fish products in Britain:

> In Trafalgar Square, a huge animated figure of a brutish sealer repeatedly clubbed an ersatz whitecoat while dozens of IFAW supporters in fuzzy white seal suits squirmed and keened on the pavement.[26]

Early in 1984, the supermarket chain Tesco responded by removing cans of Canadian salmon and herring from its shelves. Letter-writing campaigns followed, and IFAW's tactics combined with Paul Watson's dramatic escapades on his flagship *Sea Shepherd II*, which included blockading St John's harbour and the eventual ramming and confiscation of his ship, had a decisive effect. The market for seal products virtually disappeared overnight, and in 1985, twenty years after Brian Davies first went to the ice, the European Union (EU) upheld the ban on baby seal pelts for an additional four years. The seal hunt would go into decline until the mid-1990s.

Paul Watson,
Canadian founder
and president of
the Sea Shepherd
Conservation
Society, following
the inauguration
of a new multihull
named after the
French film legend
and animal rights
activist Brigitte
Bardot, 26 May
2011.

THE LINES OF BATTLE

When, in 1965, the then Minister of Fisheries, the Honourable H.
J. Robichaud, told the Canadian House of Commons that his
duty was to protect the sealing industry not the seals, Brian
Davies commented that the battle lines had been drawn. It was
the government against the whitecoats. The protests did, however,
have considerable effect on the enemy. In 1967, responding to
horrified reports from the ice and prodding from activists, the
Canadian government prohibited sealers from using the traditional gaff (a pole with a hook), and mandated the killing of seals
with a hardwood bat or a *hakapik* (the favoured instrument of
Norwegians). In 1971 the government set the first quota for the
hunt – the 'total allowable catch', or TAC. The TAC has remained a

controversial number, as it is both very difficult to count seals (which spend much of their lives in the water in the far north), and to determine at which point the population is endangered. The legislation also demanded that, prior to skinning a seal, the hunter check to ensure that the animal was indeed dead, to avoid the grisly accounts of seals skinned alive, stripped bodies writhing in agony.[27] The hunters acknowledged that there had been mistakes, but the new rules meant that they must now strike each seal three times: 'One to kill the animal, one for DFO [Department of Fisheries and Oceans], and one for Greenpeace.'[28] In 1987 the Canadian government banned the commercial harvest of whitecoats and bluebacks, and hunting from large vessels. This decision followed recommendations in the *Report of the Royal Commission on Seals and Sealing in Canada* (Malouf Report), issued in 1986.

The end of the whitecoat and blueback hunt effectively ended the fur trade in seals. For the people of the seal, the Inuit and the Newfoundlanders, it brought economic ruin. An Inuit hunter who earned about $23 for a ringed sealskin in 1976 found that after

Sealskin boots made by Rachel Uyarasuk (Iglulik, Nunavut, Canada).

Inuit skinning a ringed seal.

the protests of 1977 the same skin was worth only $4. The Inuit did not hunt for exclusively commercial reasons. They hunted seals for food, and since the mid-1950s had sold the skins to the Hudson's Bay Company, enabling northern families to participate to a limited extent in the cash economy of the south, purchasing foodstuffs, hunting equipment and domestic goods. By the mid-1980s, the annual export of seal pelts from the north had fallen by almost 97 per cent.[29] Greenlanders experienced the same loss of income, ameliorated somewhat by government subsidies for pelts. Without the income from sealskins (and other furs), many northerners lack the ability to buy southern foods or any of the comforts enjoyed by other citizens. In recent years, Inuit and Greenlanders have launched their own anti-anti-sealing campaigns. Ali Ippak from Nunavut in Canada's Arctic mused that perhaps

The only way to have people start buying skins again is to have them understand. I guess it is the only way. As Inuit we do not count how many seals we are going to catch during any period of time ... They should be made to understand it is difficult for us ... The selling of sealskins stopped because of their opposition to the massive killing of seals. We are not like that. I've said this because I think sealskins could be sold again.[30]

Fashion designers, both in the Canadian Arctic and in Greenland and Denmark, have nevertheless been incorporating sealskin in high fashion garments. Trinkets and souvenirs critiqued by IFAW and Greenpeace have largely disappeared, replaced by high quality sealskin mitts, boots and other garments.[31] The Nunavut Arts and Crafts Association sold 'SEAL is the new BLACK' T-shirts at a trade fair in Ottawa in early 2014, and provided delegates with the familiar 'twisted ribbon' for a cause. Made from sealskin, the 'Show Some Skin' ribbon urges wearers to support 'seal skin products and the Inuit way of life'. Many young Inuit do not support celebrities like Ellen DeGeneres, an actress who on her website called seal hunting 'one of the most atrocious and in-humane acts against animals allowed by any government', urging people to contribute to efforts to end the current hunt. DeGeneres donated $1.5 million of money raised from her celebrated 'selfie' tweet at the 2014 Academy Awards to the Humane Society, which opposes the seal hunt. In response, many Inuit posted 'sealfies' on their websites and on social media. On YouTube, one young Inuit woman made no apologies for eating seal meat and wearing sealskin:

While I agree with standing up for what you believe in, I also realize that [DeGeneres] didn't have all the information on the story . . . She didn't have the perspective of the indigenous peoples and their cultural views.[32]

The value of the hunt to Newfoundlanders was also both economic and cultural, but the distinction was complicated by the division between the commercial hunt, controlled out of Norway, and the hunt by landsmen. Anti-seal hunt protesters had sought to ally themselves with the Newfoundlanders and Madelinots who followed a more 'traditional' hunt from small boats, what Greenpeace saw as an alliance against larger capitalist enterprises. Brian Davies admitted a grudging admiration for the sealers he met on his first trip to the ice:

> They were poorly clad against the bitter cold. They worked at an impossible rate for long hours, their minds blanked against the slaughter. For all this killing, all this non-stop effort, they would receive only a few hundred dollars . . . They were ordinary men, earning a living as best they could, but few admitted to deriving any pleasure from their work.[33]

Individual sealers would also admit that 'there was really no joy in killing a seal . . . These seals were available and you went and got them in season'. Some would also confess that when a whitecoat looked up 'with them eyes . . . It wasn't easy'.[34] In a television interview in 1980, Davies said that the men he talked to would welcome some other form of employment: 'I mean nobody in their right mind wants to spend four or five weeks of the year beating baby seals over the head.'[35]

Paul Watson was less equivocal in his judgement of the sealers. He called the sealers of the Magdalen Islands 'barbarians' and 'Maganderthals', who he claimed were 'fuelled by a rabid malevolence born of a history of ethnic feuding and the frustrations of

the uneducated and the institutionally unemployed'.[36] Cleveland
Amory of the Fund for Animals, who had provided the money for
the first *Sea Shepherd*, was even more strident:

> I've run into one hell of a bunch of cruel bastards in my day,
> slob hunters, elephant-killers, bullfighters, bunny-bashers,
> horse-whippers, all of them thugs and cowards, every one,
> but that bunch in the Magdalen Islands – they take the
> prize for the most savage, brutal, and unforgivable acts of
> cruelty on God's green earth![37]

The Newfoundland sealers fared no better from their critics.
Watson called them ugly brutes, 'their faces smeared with blood
and contorted with rage'.[38] One of the hunt observers, a veterin-
arian, speculated that the sealers, 'killing up to 100 whitecoats a
day are brutalized by the whole procedure, and work themselves
into a state where they no longer realize what they are doing'.[39]
Sealers disagreed. As one said,

> I don't think we can connect the seal fishery as a seal hunt
> . . . It's part of a cycle in your life, as a mariner, that goes
> from one season of your life to another season, and it's
> all brought on by nature itself . . . The same boats we use
> to catch groundfish, we use to catch seals, and it's just a
> cycle.[40]

To many in the traditional fisheries, the seals were just that – fish.
Dr Arthur May explained in late 1976: 'We consider the seal the
same as seaweed – a marine resource to be harvested.'[41] A sealer
observed 'seals were like fish, were no more than cod, you know'.
To shoot at a seal was like 'firing at vegetables'. Another felt that
fishing for seal was part of nature: 'animals bleed, and there's

blood, and the thing is dead . . . The only difference between that and a turnip is that a turnip doesn't bleed.'[42] In this context the sealers' toast, 'Bloody decks and a bumper crop', is more easily understood.

It was not just that seals were considered part of the bounty of the sea to be harvested, it was that for many Newfoundlanders in the 1960s and '70s, proceeds from the seal hunt were a significant part of the family economy, roughly up to one-third of cash income in a good year.[43] Newfoundlanders were not only offended by the abusive language used by the protesters, but appalled by the ready condemnation of those who had evidently never experienced want. As one woman wrote to a St John's newspaper in March 1977,

> Tell me, Miss Bardot, do you recall at lamplight melting ice with your breath from the kitchen window? Yes, ten tiny faces peeping through, looking, waiting anxiously for a dad long overdue from the seal hunt, risking his life (for you) hopping from pan of ice to pan of ice in deathly chilling waters for barely enough money to buy molasses and tea.[44]

They were also profoundly disturbed by the dismissal of their history of hardship and living by the sea. The St John's *Evening Telegram* called the campaign 'A hatchet job . . . The image of the Province is being smeared falsely and viciously.' Another article added 'We will not let anybody from anywhere do anything that would destroy our traditional values . . . We're fighting for our very survival in Newfoundland.' The Newfoundland Premier Frank Moores contended that the protesters 'should be arrested' but with sly Newfoundland humour suggested that for punishment they should be 'made to eat overripe seal meat three times a day for 30 days. Then they should be dipped in a vat of perman-ent pink dye and shipped off home.'[45] The last was a reference to Greenpeace's plan to mark the seal pups with green dye. Pink was also perhaps a reference to the posturing of the eco-warriors.

Newfoundlanders, dab hands at protest themselves, founded Codpeace, a pro-seal hunt group, in 1979. Its motto was 'In Cod We Trust' and its mascot Cuddles the Cod. Created by Miller Ayre, a Newfoundland businessman, the Codpeace Foundation sought protection for the cod, offering training to young New-foundlanders willing to place their bodies between that of a cod and a ravenous seal. They also sought funding for a march on Washington, where they would threaten to attack the 'Great Seal of the United States'. Their spokespeople, Dr Cod O'Gratin, Jacques Codstew and the Codfather, appeared at public events urging viewers to write to politicians to protect the adorable baby cod. Cuddles the Cod himself would also appear in public (a costumed member of Codpeace) to the accompaniment of The Codpeace Song (sung to the tune of The Ode to Newfoundland):

How can you be so cod-descending
The protest groups slander us with such seal
They cry that the harp is so helpless and lovely
Don't you know the coddle is their favourite meal
On the surface they might look real cute and cuddly
But deep down underneath they're savage and cruel.
Oh, the sea it is filled with the tears and sad stories
Heartbroken codfathers, codmothers too.[46]

Despite the humour, the seal hunt protests unsettled New-foundlanders and did have a significant effect on the traditional culture of the outports. The collapse of the cod stock in the early 1990s, the result of decades of commercial overfishing, left

Newfoundlanders and all those who lived by the harvest of the North Atlantic with fewer and fewer links to a way of life that had developed over centuries.

From 1984 until 1994 an uneasy truce took hold between the opponents of the seal hunt and the sealing industry. During that period, the industry and the government sought new markets, particularly in Asia. In 1995, with populations of harp, hood and grey seals growing and the cod fishery under threat, the Canadian government set the quota for the hunt (TAC) at 250,000 seals. The quota was raised to 350,000 by 2004. The seal wars had begun again. Observers from IFAW saw and reported abuses on the ice, and a new generation of anti-seal hunt protesters began to react in horror to scenes of bloody carcasses and men clubbing seals. The government maintained that the seal hunt was 'the most humane in the world' and officials had indeed worked with sealers and the industry to improve equipment and training. Sealers themselves credited the earlier debates and protests with encouraging respect for the animals, and for training 'proper sealers' who worked in a professional manner.[47] What neither sealers nor governments could change, however, was the perception of sealing as 'the most brutal hunt in the world'.[48] They were not helped in their efforts by the comments of politicians like John Efford, the Newfoundland and Labrador Minister of Fisheries and Aquaculture:

> I would like to see the 6 million seals, or whatever number is out there, killed and sold, or destroyed or burned. I do not care what happens to them . . . the more they kill the better I will love it.[49]

Despite the fact that it had been illegal to kill whitecoats since 1987, new celebrities came to the ice for pictures with baby seals, from Pamela Anderson to Sir Paul McCartney.[50] Even Brigitte Bardot returned to Canada in 2006 for what she thought would be her last visit, with a plea to stop the 'barbaric massacre'.[51] Opponents also cited the declining economic importance of the hunt, trumpeting its dependence on subsidies and government support to maintain even the small markets for seal oil, furs and body parts. In 2013 Rebecca Aldworth of Humane Society International claimed that as a result of failing markets, the Canadian government had repeatedly subsidized Carino, the Newfoundland-based subsidiary of G. C. Rieber, the Norwegian fur and food products company. She lambasted an industry 'limping along on credit and subsidies', which Sheryl Fink of IFAW also insisted had been on life support for twenty years.[52] In 2014 Canada and Norway, supported by Inuit Tapiriit Kanatami (ITK), lost their appeal to the World Trade Organization 'on public moral grounds' to overturn the European ban on imported seal products, though allowance was made for products from Inuit hunters.[53] The quota for the 2014 hunt was 400,000 seals, the same as in 2013, but less than one-fifth was landed, and the anti-seal hunt campaigners celebrated that the hunt was in its last days. Just as the protest still raises the hackles of those far from the ice, the counter protest finds new supporters in surprising places. Celebrity chef Anthony Bourdain ate raw seal with the Inuit in Quebec, and criticized his colleagues who signed a petition to stop using Canadian seafood until the seal hunt ended.[54] Bourdain's concern was for the welfare and future of the Inuit. In Newfoundland and Quebec, chefs who grew up eating seal are combining culinary traditions with the new gastronomy of the Nose to Tail school. They have found seal a versatile meat that goes far beyond flipper pie, appearing on menus raw or smoked, as jerky or burgers; seal oil is even a flavour of ice cream.

While the seal wars may be coming to a close, they are not over, and they are moving to a new battleground. The collapse of the North Atlantic fish stocks at the end of the twentieth century has revived the old rivalry between the seals and the fishers. When catches plummet, fishers look for the culprit, and seals are fish-eaters. Harbour, harp or grey seal, all have been accused of decimating the fish – cod, herring, salmon – on which livelihoods depend. In Britain, complaints about grey seals began in the 1930s, and by the 1970s Greenpeace was intervening to stop the culls in Scotland.[55] It is unfortunate that seal populations appear to rise as fish populations fall, and it is hard for many, including politicians, not to draw the obvious conclusion. Harold Theriault, a member of the Nova Scotia Legislature, was seemingly horrified by the potential reproductive capacity of the grey seals off the coast:

> These grey seals, Mr Speaker, don't need the ice to have their babies on, they just slide up the beach anywhere and have a baby; they can slide up on the street and have a baby . . . They're out here in the harbour right now and they'll be up on the streets of Halifax if they keep accumulating – and I don't know how these fish stocks are standing it inshore . . . They've got to go and find the food, so watch out, they're coming up these streets.[56]

Added to Theriault's concern about the depredations on cod and salmon is an almost primordial fear of multitudes emerging from the deep, the dread-eyed seals spawning on land, the selkie coming for his bride.

WHY WHITECOATS?

The seal hunt and its mascot, the whitecoat, are arguably among the most potent environmental symbols in the world. Anti-seal hunt organizations like the Humane Society and IFAW continue to fan the flames of indignation and distress with the touching image of the helpless baby seal.[57] Jacques Cousteau famously said,

> The harp seal question is entirely emotional. We have to be logical. We have to aim our activity first to the endangered species. Those who are moved by the plight of the harp seal could also be moved by the plight of the pig . . .

Marzipan seals for sale in Lubeck.

We have to be logical. If we are sentimental about harp seals, which are not endangered because they are partially protected, then we have to also be emotional about pigs.[58]

His comparison was not appreciated by the anti-seal hunt campaigners. The baby seal was not comparable to a piglet. The whitecoat evokes in many people a strong protective response.[59] Brigitte Bardot wrote after her encounter on the ice:

The baby seals look at us confidently with their big, soulful eyes. I take one in my arms. I kiss his wet nose and my tears join his.

Suddenly, the mother seal's head appears, and her cries beckon the baby. She gives me a quizzical look, discovering me kissing her baby. Could she be jealous? I'm sorry, Mama Seal, but I will spend my life fighting for him.[60]

The uncanny sense of familiarity with sealdom informs our relations with the whitecoats. The American science-fiction writer Ray Bradbury acknowledged the 'signal' that flashed from their eyes: 'Something of my soul fires from that gaze, deny it as I might.'[61] But it is not just the old ties between seal and humankind that have made the whitecoat such a potent icon. The baby seal with the look of a helpless puppy might be described, as George Allan England did, as 'great white or whitish-yellow pincushions, woggling along, lying still, taking their blobby and fullfed ease, heaving around'.[62] Or they might be seen, as Sir Wilfred Grenfell saw them, as holy innocents. In preaching to the Inuit, he sought to convey the 'Oriental similes of the Bible':

The whitecoat also provides comfort for people with dementia. PARO is a Japanese-designed therapeutic robot seal.

A white-coated harp seal pup on ice in the North Atlantic.

Thus the Lamb of God had to be translated kotik or young seal. This animal, with its perfect whiteness as it lies in its cradle of ice, its gentle, helpless nature, and its pathetic innocent eyes, is probably as apt a substitute . . . as nature offers.[63]

Take the charm of resemblance, add to it the proportion of a baby's face, and place it at the heart of the purest landscape imaginable to the western imagination, then club it to bloody death, and the power of the whitecoat is evident.

Whether one sympathizes with the sealers, or sides with the seals, we cannot but help acknowledge our ancient history together. As Ray Bradbury wrote:

Somewhere far back down the line, our hearts and blood moved much the same. Some old racial memory lost in me remembers this. It is hard for me to look and not read the bright signals. I hear the old heartbeat from a million-plus years ago.

Their family, my family, our family, are here gazing at one another . . . I cannot refuse the stare that asks great questions that must be answered. I cannot turn away.[64]

Timeline of the Seal

c. 350	1494	1638	1741	1758
Aristotle describes the seal in *History of Animals*	Christopher Columbus encounters the Caribbean monk seal	Naturalist Ulisse Aldrovandi observes a trained seal in Europe	George Anson and his crew discover the southern elephant seal on the Juan Fernandez Islands	Linnaeus describes the harbour seal and the southern elephant seal in *Systema naturae*

1922	1928	1932	1941	1961
Mexican government bans elephant seal hunting, followed by the U.S. government in 1923	John Ringling buys two elephant seals for his circus, and names them Goliath I and II	Both Ringling Goliaths die in captivity	Naturalist Ronald Lockley meets the grey seals of the Godir in Wales	Andre the seal adopted by Harry Goodridge

1977	1979	1982	1985	1989
Brigitte Bardot kisses her first baby seal	Newfoundlanders found 'Codpeace' in response to anti-seal hunt protests	European Economic Community bans import of baby seal skins	Obituary for Hoover the harbour seal appears in the *Boston Globe*	Maruko, the southern elephant seal, becomes a 'guest' at Futami Sea Paradise in Japan

3	1859	1892	1894	1914

3

nter seal
nt begins in
wfoundland

1859

Jenny, the 'Talking and Performing Fish', amuses Londoners, while Ned and Fanny, the 'learned seals', entertain Bostonians

1892

Museum collectors shoot seven of the eight remaining northern elephant seals on Guadalupe Island

1894

Rudyard Kipling pens the seals' sad National Anthem in *The Jungle Book*

1914

Great Newfoundland sealing disaster

The Grey Seals Protection Act offers partial protection for seal populations in the UK

4

e film *Les
nds Phoques
a banquise
tes seal hunt
troversy

1969

Brian Davies founds the International Fund for Animal Welfare (IFAW)

1971

George and Alice Swallow adopt Hoover, the 'Talking Seal'

1972

Convention for the Conservation of Antarctic Seals adopted by the signatories to the Antarctic Treaty

7

covery of *Puijila darwini*
researchers from
adian Museum of
ure in Canada's Arctic

2009

Terrie Williams acquires the Hawaiian monk seal KP2

2014

The EU upholds ban on imported North American seal products (with exceptions for Inuit hunters)

Inuit post 'sealfies' online in protest of Ellen DeGeneres's donation to the Humane Society

References

INTRODUCTION

1 The Benedictine monk Mavro Vetranović lived for 40 years on a small island off the Dalmation coast, where he confronted the 'sea bears'. Cited in William M. Johnson, 'Monk Seals in Post-classical History: The Role of the Mediterranean Monk Seal (*Monachus monachus*)', in *European History and Culture, from the Fall of Rome to the 20th Century* (Nederlandsche Commissie Voor Internationale Natuurbescherming, Mededelingen No. 39, 2004), pp. 35–6.
2 Quoted in Robert Hamilton, 'The Natural History of the Amphibious Carnivora', in *The Naturalist's Library: Mammalia*, VIII (Edinburgh, 1839), pp. 121–2.
3 'While they are trapped within the bay they often go along the shore letting themselves be seen without any fear, showing by certain actions they make that they understand everything that is said to them.' Quoted in Johnson, 'Monk Seals in Post-classical History', p. 36.

1 TRUE SEALS

1 Victor B. Scheffer, *Seals, Sea Lions and Walruses: A Review of the Pinnipedia* (Stanford, CA, 1958), p. 52.
2 Quoted in Marianne Riedman, *The Pinnipeds: Seals, Sea Lions and Walruses* (Berkeley, CA, 1990), p. 1.
3 Natalia Rybczynski, Mary R. Dawson and Richard H. Tedford, 'A Semi-aquatic Arctic Mammalian Carnivore from the

Miocene Epoch and Origin of Pinnipedia', *Nature*, CDLVIII
(23 April 2009), pp. 1021–4; www.nature.com, accessed
16 January 2014.

4 Charles Darwin, *On the Origin of Species by Means of Natural
Selection* (London, 1872), p. 224.

5 The climate of the Arctic 23 million years ago was considerably
warmer than it is today, and Mary Dawson (a member of the
2007 Devon Island team) also found a fossil rhinoceros on an
expedition in 1985. Canadian Museum of Nature, 'Puijila,
A Prehistoric Walking Seal', www.nature.ca, accessed
20 January 2014.

6 Joel Asaph Allen, *A History of North American Pinnipeds:
A Monograph of the Walruses, Sea-lions, Sea-bears and Seals
of North America* (Washington, DC, 1880), quoted in Scheffer,
Seals, Sea Lions and Walruses, p. 52.

7 Marianne Riedman recounts the story of a misguided fur seal
who took to the streets of San Francisco and twice entered a
men's washroom in the same building. Riedman, *The Pinnipeds*,
p. 12.

8 Aristotle, *On the Parts of Animals I–IV*, trans. James Lennox
(Oxford, 2002), p. 38.

9 William M. Johnson and David M. Lavigne also suggest that
'phoca may have Hebraic origins, its Greek meaning defined as
"one who walks with difficulty"', see 'Monk Seals in Antiquity:
The Mediterranean Monk Seal (*Monachus monachus*)', in
Ancient History and Literature (Nederlandsche Commissie Voor
Internationale Natuurbescherming, Mededelingen No. 35, 1999),
p. 3, n. 4.

10 Robert Hamilton, 'The Natural History of the Amphibious
Carnivora', in *The Naturalist's Library*: *Mammalia*, VIII
(Edinburgh, 1839), p. 68.

11 Riedman, *The Pinnipeds*, p. 16.

12 Estimates are from 7 million to 75 million, a range that
reflects the difficulty of population census in the frozen seas.
See C. Southwell (IUCN SSC Pinniped Specialist Group) 2008.

Lobodon carcinophaga. The IUCN Red List of Threatened Species. Version 2015.2; www.iucnredlist.org, accessed 1 July 2015.

13 The French naturalist Johann Hermann gave the monk seal its scientific name in 1779, derived from its supposed resemblance, when seen from behind, to a monk: 'In this posture, it looked from the rear not dissimilar to a black monk, in the way that its smooth round head resembled a human head covered by a hood, and its shoulders, with the short, outstretched feet, imagined like two elbows protruding from a scapular, from which a long, unfolded, black robe flows down.' See 'The Curious Case of the Monk Seal – Why Monk?' (December 2012), www.monachus-guardian.org, accessed 26 January 2014.

14 A. Aguilar and L. Lowry (IUCN SSC Pinniped Specialist Group) 2013. *Monachus monachus*. The IUCN Red List of Threatened Species, Version 2015.2; www.iucnredlist.org, accessed 1 July 2015.

15 Quoted in Allen, *History of North American Pinnipeds*, pp. 715, 721.

16 NOAA Fisheries, Pacific Island Region, Protected Resources Division, 'Hawaiian Monk Seal', www.nmfs.noaa.gov, accessed 12 December 2014.

17 A. R. Hoelzel et al., 'Elephant Seal Genetic Variation and the Use of Simulation Models to Investigate Historical Population Bottlenecks', *Journal of Heredity*, LXXXIV (1993), pp. 443–9 (p. 445).

18 Burney Le Boeuf, 'The Aggression of the Breeding Bulls', *Natural History*, CXXX (1971), pp. 82–94 (p. 85).

19 George Anson, *A Voyage Around the World, in the Years MDCCXL, I, II, III, IV*, vol. I (Edinburgh, 1781), p. 137.

20 Noted in Hamilton, 'Natural History of the Amphibious Carnivora', p. 211.

21 Quoted ibid., p. 235.

22 Le Boeuf, 'The Aggression of the Breeding Bulls', p. 87.

23 Anson, *Voyage Around the World*, p. 138.

24 Scheffer, *Seals, Sea Lions and Walruses*, p. 123.

25 The other lobodontine seals also have specialized krill-straining teeth.

26 Riedman, *The Pinnipeds*, p. 149.

27 From an account of the Shackleton expedition by Alfred Lansing, *Endurance* (1959), quoted ibid., pp. 158–9.

28 Nor was a British scientist who was attacked and killed by a leopard seal in December 2014. 'Horror in the Antarctic as Giant Seal Kills Scientist', *Daily Mail* (14 December 2014), www.dailymail.co.uk.

29 T. Härkönen (IUCN SSC Pinniped Specialist Group) 2008. *Pusa caspica*. The IUCN Red List of Threatened Species. Version 2015.2; www.iucnredlist.org, accessed 1 July 2015.

30 Subspecies of ringed seal also exist in freshwater lakes in Russia and Finland, and harbour seals inhabit freshwater lakes in Canada.

31 Though this has been questioned: see Nigel Bonner, *Seals of the World* (London, 1999), p. 167.

32 Riedman, *The Pinnipeds*, p. 243.

33 Carl Linnaeus, *Systema naturae per regna tria naturæ*, 10th edn, I (Stockholm, 1758). Quotation cited in Scheffer, *Seals, Sea Lions and Walruses*, p. 3.

34 Fisheries and Oceans Canada, 'Aquatic Species at Risk – Harbour Seal Lacs des Loups Marins subspecies', www.dfo-mpo.gc.ca, accessed 20 January 2014.

35 Michael Carroll, *The Seal and Herring Fisheries of Newfoundland: Together with a Condensed History of the Island* (Montreal, 1873), p. 11.

36 Allen, *History of North American Pinnipeds*, pp. 485–6.

37 Hamilton, 'Natural History of the Amphibious Carnivora', p. 219.

38 Whitlow W. L. Au and Mardi C. Hastings, *Principles of Marine Bioacoustics* (Springer e-book, 2008), p. 473.

39 Riedman, *The Pinnipeds*, pp. 331–2.

40 Quoted in Hamilton, 'Natural History of the Amphibious Carnivora', p. 77.

41 Rowena Farre, *Seal Morning* (Leicester, nd), p. 32.

42 As well as other more exotic fare – one leopard seal was found
   off the coast of Australia with a duckbill platypus in the stomach.

43 George Brown Goode, *The Fisheries and Fishery Industries of the
   United States*, Section I Text (Washington, DC, 1884), p. 60.

44 Darren Naish,'Harbour Seal Kills and Eats Duck', in Tetrapod
   Zoology blog, 6 March 2009, http://scienceblogs.com.

45 A nineteenth-century sealer averred that 'The milk of all breeding
   seals is of the consistency of white paint'; cited in Carroll, *Seal
   and Herring Fisheries of Newfoundland*, p. 26.

46 Riedman, *The Pinnipeds*, p. 276.

47 Ibid., p. 270.

48 Carroll, *Seal and Herring Fisheries of Newfoundland*, pp. 25–6.

49 Allen, *History of North American Pinnipeds*, p. 649.

50 Carroll, *Seal and Herring Fisheries of Newfoundland*, p. 25.

51 Allen, *History of North American Pinnipeds*, p. 754.

52 Aristotle, *The History of Animals*, Book II, Part 1; Book VI, Part 12,
   http://classics.mit.edu, accessed 20 January 2014.

53 Aristotle also noted that seals resembled serpents in their
   'split-tongues'. Ibid., Book II, Part 1. Seals indeed have tongues
   split at the tips.

54 Allen, *History of North American Pinnipeds*, p. 493.

55 Ibid., p. 494.

56 T. C. Chambert, J. J. Rotella and R. A. Garrott, 'Environmental
   Extremes Versus Ecological Extremes: Impact of a Massive
   Iceberg on the Population Dynamics of a High-level Antarctic
   Marine Predator', *Proceedings of the Royal Society B: Biological
   Sciences*, CCLXXIX (2012), pp. 4532–41.

57 Allen, *History of North American Pinnipeds*, pp. 489–90. The IUCN
   estimates the global harp seal population at 8 million animals.

2 SEALS AND PEOPLE

  1 Francis Galton, 'The First Steps Towards the Domestication of
    Animals', http://galton.org, accessed 3 October 2014, pp. 13–14.
    A later observer also recorded the expulsion of a seal from the

human home for stealing milk from the cows: 'That one in particular became so tame that he lay along the fire among the dogs, bathed in the sea, and returned to the house; but having found his way to the byres, used to steal there unobserved and suck the cows; on this account he was discharged, and sent to his native element.' Noted in Robert Hamilton, 'The Natural History of the Amphibious Carnivora', in *The Naturalist's Library*: *Mammalia*, viii (Edinburgh, 1839), p. 134.

2 The farmer offered it for sale, because, as an editorial in the local paper said: 'a seal about the premises is pretty noisome, dead or alive and about the best thing one can do with a seal caught in a bag is to turn it loose on a beach and push it into the spacious Pacific'. From 'The Fretful Porcupine', *The Observer*, 16 August 1913, http://circuszooanimals.blogspot.ca, accessed 3 October 2014.

3 Seals have been called sea-calves, sea-oxen, even sea-bullock, but these names refer as much to their lowing and grunting as to their metaphorical affinity to the domesticated beasts of the land.

4 Quoted in Hamilton, 'Natural History of the Amphibious Carnivora', pp. 287–8.

5 Ibid, p. 172.

6 Rowena Farre, *Seal Morning* (Leicester, nd), p. 172.

7 'Nevertheless they learn what is taught them; and they salute the People at the same Time with the Voice and Look; the Sound being a rude Murmuring. If called by their Name, they answer.' Pliny the Elder, *Natural History*, ix (15), http://data.perseus.org, accessed 2 February 2014.

8 Oppian, 'Halieutica', v, 35–8, in *Oppian, Colluthus, Tryphiodorus*, English trans. by A. W. Mair (London, 1928), p. 463, available at https://archive.org, accessed 2 February 2014.

9 William M. Johnson, 'Monk Seals in Post-classical History: The Role of the Mediterranean Monk Seal (*Monachus monachus*)', in *European History and Culture, from the Fall of Rome to the 20th Century* (Nederlandsche Commissie Voor Internationale Natuurbescherming, Mededelingen No. 39, 2004), p. 57.

10 Ibid., p. 58.

11 Quoted in Hamilton, 'Natural History of the Amphibious Carnivora', pp. 287–8.

12 Her trainer savvily offered 'Complimentary cards to naturalists and gentlemen of the press . . . issued for private performances three days before public exhibition'. The Cat's Meat Shop blog, 15 September 2010, http://catsmeatshop.blogspot.ca, accessed 1 April 2014.

13 Francis Buckland, *Curiosities of Natural History*, Fourth Series (London, 1888; 2008), p. 128. Was Buckland suggesting that seal language 'may be said to resemble our own'? Curious indeed. In the 1870 edition of *Curiosities*, Buckland also referred to a seal named Jemmy and her partner Jack who performed similar actions, but apparently did not talk (p. 173).

14 'Boston Zoological and Aquarial Gardens', in *Ballou's Dollar Monthly Magazine*, XVI, 1 July 1862, pp. 1–16 (pp. 7–8).

15 'Généralement le phoque des baraques élyséennes, au bout de deux ou trois ans d'exercice, est forcé d'abandonner sa profession pour donner tous ses soins à la guérison de ses rhumatismes.' (Generally, after two or three years of this exercise, the seal of the Elysée is forced to abandon the profession to devote all his efforts to curing his rheumatism.) Edmond Texier, *Tableau de Paris*, I (Paris, 1852), p. 18.

16 'Captain' Joseph Woodward began his career working with a trained seal, but became famous as a circus and music-hall entertainer working with sea lions, who proved more 'useful'. He was recruited by the Admiralty during the First World War to train the mammals as submarine trackers. D.A.H. Wilson, 'Sea Lions, Greasepaint and the U-boat Threat: Admiralty Scientists Turn to the Music Hall in 1916', Royal Society Publishing, 22 September 2001, http://royalsocietypublishing.org, accessed 4 October 2014.

17 John R. Coryell, 'The Largest Pet in the World', *St Nicholas: An Illustrated Magazine for Young Folks*, X/2 (May–October 1883), pp. 933–7 (p. 935).

18 In 1911 six young northern elephant seals were captured live for the New York Aquarium, but lived for only two years.

19 From a post-mortem account in 1932, www.collectorsweekly.com, accessed 10 February 2014.

20 Albert Tucker, 'Two Monsters of the Old Ringling Circus Recalled', *Sarasota Herald-Tribune* (30 December 1962), p. 6; http://news.google.com, accessed 10 February 2014.

21 'Roland of the Berlin Zoo', Pathé Films, 1931; www.britishpathe.com, accessed 12 February 2014.

22 There are currently 445 seals in zoological parks, aquaria and marine parks worldwide (species data provided by International Species Information System or ISIS, personal communication). Many also provide rescue services for orphaned pups and injured animals. Sea Life, 'The World's Largest Aquarium Brand', supports two seal sanctuaries in the UK, with the aim of 'rescue, rehabilitation and release'. The Vancouver Aquarium has a special Marine Mammal Rescue Centre, and admits anywhere from 100 to 150 injured or ill harbour seals each year, with the goal of returning the animals back to the wild. Specialized seal rescue centres also exist almost anywhere that people interact with seals, from the Orkneys to the Netherlands (*Zeehondencreche*, or seal sanctuary) to the coasts of California.

23 Feisty, the ageing and nearly blind harbour seal at the Lake Superior Zoo, became a spokeseal for a different cause. In June 2012, when flooding released him from his pool, he was found swimming the streets of Duluth, Minnesota. He became an Internet sensation, the face of the flood. Timothy Blotz, 'Feisty the Seal: Anatomy of a Duluth Flood Meme', Stand By . . . blog, 22 June 2012, http://timothyblotz.com.

24 'National Zoo Seal Pup is too Cute!', WUSA, 5 February 2014, www.wusa9.com; 'Ridiculously Cute Grey Seal Pup Born at Brookfield Zoo', The Pet Collective website, 7 January 2014, www.thepetcollective.tv.

25 'Elephant Seal Marks Longevity Record in Captivity', Asahi Shimbun, 10 September 2012, http://ajw.asahi.com, accessed 1 April 2014.

26 Quoted in Hamilton, 'Natural History of the Amphibious Carnivora', pp. 287–8.

27 Farre, *Seal Morning*, p. 174.

28 Stan Carey, Sentence First, an Irishman's blog about the English language, 26 January 2010, http://stancarey.wordpress.com, accessed 15 February 2014.

29 In addition to the engraved image of George and Hoover together, George Swallow's headstone also bears the inscription, 'Keep out of the hot sun, don't take any wooden nickels', advice Hoover's grandson, Chacoda, who inherited his vocal ability, might well heed. Chacoda's complex name is made up of Chauncy (a lobster pier in Maine that a lot of trainers enjoyed) and Coda (the end of a musical piece, since Chacoda's mother is named Trumpet), but most people call him simply Chuck; http://trainers.neaq.org, accessed 3 October 2014.

30 Hoover the Talking Seal Obituary, www.findagrave.com, accessed 20 February 2014.

31 Harry Goodridge and Lew Dietz, *A Seal called Andre: The Two Worlds of a Maine Harbour Seal* (New York, 1975), p. 4.

32 Ibid., p. 8.

33 Ibid., p. 32.

34 Ibid., p. 3.

35 Ibid., p. 11.

36 The canny Passamaquoddy Indians made a business out of crafting many seal 'noses' from a single skin, so the cull may have been somewhat less than surmised.

37 Goodridge and Dietz, *A Seal called Andre*, p. 176.

38 Kai Curry-Lindahl, Review of *Grey Seal, Common Seal* by R. M. Lockley, in *Journal of Wildlife Management*, xxxii/3 (July 1968), pp. 651–3.

39 Ken Jones, *Seal Doctor: The Delightful Story of Ken Jones and his Orphan Seals* (Glasgow, 1978), p. 114.

40 The Vancouver Aquarium Marine Mammal Rescue Centre considers seals as 'patients', and releases status updates on individual seals, the majority named after elements on the

periodic table, but some with more appealing monikers – 'Southside Johnny', 'Conway Twitty' and 'Tina Turner' among them; www.vanaqua.org, accessed 13 October 2014.

41 Goodridge and Dietz, *A Seal called Andre*, p. 172.

42 Ewan Clarkson, *Halic: The Story of a Grey Seal* (New York, 1970; 1971), p. 158. Halic's name is derived from the species name, *Halichoerus grypus*. Despite the title and content of Clarkson's book, the paperback cover bears the portrait of a sea lion, flippers tucked under.

43 R. M. Lockley, *The Saga of the Grey Seal: Introducing the Natural History of the Grey Seal of the North Atlantic* (New York, 1955), p. 5.

44 Ibid., p. 55.

45 Ibid., pp. 126–7.

46 Ibid., p. 32. See chapter Four, p. 120, for an account of Ronald Lockley's novel, *Seal-Woman*.

47 Terrie Williams, *The Odyssey of KP2: An Orphan Seal, A Marine Biologist and the Fight to Save a Species* (New York, 2012), p. 15.

48 Ibid., p. 2.

49 'Captain' Woodward, the sea-lion trainer, opined 'It is all done by fish and patience, and I put fish first'; see Wilson, 'Sea Lions', www.townteasers.co.uk, accessed 4 October 2014.

50 Williams, *Odyssey of KP2*, p. 127.

51 Lockley, *Saga of the Grey Seal*, p. 21.

52 Williams, *Odyssey of KP2*, pp. 148–9.

53 The plaque reads: 'NELSON Obit 2003. A distinctive "one-eyed" scarred bull Grey Seal (Halichoerus Grypus) who was a familiar sight in the harbours of south Cornwall for over 25 years. Eventually he settled on the rocks of Looe Island as his home and made Looe harbour his dining room where he was fed and his company enjoyed by local fishermen, townsfolk and countless visitors. "A Grand Old Man of the Sea" and a great favourite with all. In life, Nelson was a splendid ambassador for his species; now, in bronze, he serves as a potent symbol of the rich marine environment of the area and a permanent reminder of the need for it to be cherished. Unveiled by Sir Robin Knox-Johnston CBE,

28th May 2008'; www.suesseals.eclipse.co.uk, accessed
28 February 2014.

54 Williams, *Odyssey of KP2*, p. 2.

55 Lono, 'KP2 Rap', trans. Terrie Williams,
www.savemonkseals.ucsc.edu, accessed 28 February 2014.

56 Rudyard Kipling, 'The White Seal', in *The Jungle Book*,
www.gutenberg.org, accessed 1 April 2014. The Pet Collective,
a website for pet lovers, posted the story of Nafanya, another seal
of a different colour. A 'ginger' or albino fur seal, she was rescued
by a wildlife photographer from the neglect of her own kind;
www.thepetcollective.tv, accessed 1 May 2014.

3 PEOPLES OF THE SEAL

1 Homer, *The Odyssey*, trans. Robert Fagles (New York, 1996), p. 138.

2 Phocaean coins minted in the seventh and sixth centuries BPE
bear the image of a seal.

3 The story is not in the biblical text, but is recounted in William
M. Johnson and David M. Lavigne, 'Monk Seals in Antiquity: The
Mediterranean Monk Seal (*Monachus monachus*)', in *Ancient
History and Literature* (Nederlandsche Commissie Voor
Internationale Natuurbescherming, Mededelingen No. 35, 1999).

4 William M. Johnson, 'Monk Seals in Post-classical History:
The Role of the Mediterranean Monk Seal (*Monachus monachus*)',
in *European History and Culture, from the Fall of Rome to the 20th
Century* (Nederlandsche Commissie Voor Internationale
Natuurbescherming, Mededelingen No. 39, 2004), pp. 20, 33–4, 44.

5 Noted in Robert Hamilton, 'The Natural History of the
Amphibious Carnivora', in *The Naturalist's Library: Mammalia*,
VIII (Edinburgh, 1839), p. 332; Johnson, 'Monk Seals in Post-
classical History', p. 79; David Thomson, *The People of the Sea:
Celtic Tales of the Seal-Folk* (Edinburgh, 1954; 1996; digital edition,
2009), p. 5.

6 Johnson notes the seals' lament for human misfortune, in
Johnson and Lavigne, 'Monk Seals in Antiquity', p. 8. Their

expressions of emotion are also noted in R. M. Lockley, *The Saga of the Grey Seal: Introducing the Natural History of the Grey Seal of the North Atlantic* (New York, 1955), p. 39.

7 Aelian, quoted in Johnson and Lavigne, 'Monk Seals in Antiquity', p. 9.

8 'I often heard the selchie babies cryin – in the autumn time. On the Skerries yonder. There's no way to tell they make from the sound o' a human baby.' Quoted in Thomson, *People of the Sea*, p. 137.

9 Aristotle evidently had the opportunity to dissect a female seal, and he noted that 'in respect of its genital organ also the female resembles a cow; in all other respects [that is, in its sexual anatomy] it resembles the human female'. Cited in Johnson and Lavigne, 'Monk Seals in Antiquity', p. 67.

10 Quoted in Johnson, 'Monk Seals in Post-classical History', p. 82.

11 Plutarch, *De sollertia animalium*, vol. XII, Loeb Classical Library edition, 1957, http://penelope.uchicago.edu, accessed 12 March 2014.

12 Nonnus, *Dionysiaca*, XXXIX, quoted in Johnson and Lavigne, 'Monk Seals in Antiquity', p. 17.

13 To the Greeks, seals also smelled far worse than goats. One of Aristophanes' ripest insults was to say that someone smelled like a seal. See Johnson and Lavigne, 'Monk Seals in Antiquity', pp. 17–18.

14 See discussion in Johnson, 'Monk Seals in Post-classical History', pp. 22–3.

15 Aristotle, *On the Gait of Animals*, Part 19, http://classics.mit.edu, and *On the History of Animals II*, Part 6, http://classics.mit.edu, both accessed 1 March 2014.

16 Johnson and Lavigne, 'Monk Seals in Antiquity', p. 20.

17 Ibid., p. 20.

18 Aristotle, *History of Animals*, cited in Johnson and Lavigne, p. 68, 18–26. There are, however, tales among the Greeks of tribes of people – the 'fish-eaters' – living along the shores of the Red Sea, who shared their livelihoods with seals, even living among them,

'just as if an untransgressible treaty had been settled between them and the seals, neither themselves plunder the seals nor are these hurt by them But each race protects their hunts without plotting against one another.' Aristotle, *History of Animals*, quoted in Johnson and Lavigne, 'Monk Seals in Antiquity', p. 66.

19 'The life of a wild animal always has a tragic end'; Ernest Thompson Seton, *Introduction to Wild Animals I Have Known*, www.gutenberg.org, accessed 30 March 2014.

20 Sule Skerry is a small rocky island remote even from the Orkneys, off the north coast of Scotland, today a Special Protection Area for seabirds. This version of the song begins 'In Norway land there lived a maid'; www.educationscotland.gov.uk. The song is still sung by folk singers and is taught in Scottish schools.

21 Melanie Jackson, *The Selkie Bride* (New York, 2010), pp. 26–7.

22 'Seal House', in Duncan Williamson, *Tales of the Seal People: Scottish Folk Tales* (Northampton, MA, 2000), p. 111.

23 Eric Linklater, 'Sealskin Trousers', in *The Goose Girl and Other Stories* (Bloomsbury Reader digital edition), pp. 42–3.

24 Ibid., p. 50.

25 Retold from Susan Cooper, *The Selkie Girl* (New York, 1986).

26 'Das Seehundsfell', *Isländische Märchen und Volkssagen* (Berlin, 1919), pp. 258–9. Translation from Icelandic into German by Åge Avenstrup and Elisabeth Treitel; trans. from German into English by D. L. Ashliman, 2000; www.pitt.edu, accessed 12 March 2014.

27 Eliza Keary, 'Little Seal-skin', in *Little Seal-skin and Other Poems* (London, 1874), pp. 1–11, p. 5.

28 'Some folk swam/ before they walked, they say, like his first girlfriend/ with her lucken toes – said/ to bring good fortune, show/ that seal-blood sang in the veins.' Excerpt from Robin Robertson, 'Selkie', quoted in Masaya Shimokusu, 'An Irish "Selkie": Robin Robertson's "Selkie" Dedicated to Michael Donaghy', http://doors.doshisha.ac.jp, accessed 17 March 2014.

29 In 1895 the Folklore Society studied magic lantern slides of Baubi Urquhart of the Shetland Islands, who attributed her seal-like appearance to selkie ancestry. Noted in Carole Silver, '"East of the

Sun, West of the Moon": Victorians and Fairy Brides', *Tulsa Studies in Women's Literature*, VI/2 (Autumn 1987), pp. 283–98 (p. 292).

30 W. Traill Dennison, *The Scottish Antiquary, or, Northern Notes and Queries*, VII/28 (1893), pp. 171–7; www.jstor.org, accessed 17 March 2014.

31 R. M Lockley, *Seal-Woman* (New York, 1975), p. 59.

32 Ibid., p. 80.

33 The theme of the seal-woman who returns to the sea was used by American Jungian analyst Clarissa Pinkola Estés as an archetype for what she calls the 'wild soul'. The woman who gives up her soul to become wife and mother must eventually return to herself – to the spiritual sea – else she wither and die. Not even the love for her child can keep her from the return, but she leaves her son with the gift of song and magic, and his people with the legend of the human-hearted seal. 'Sealskin, Soulskin', in Clarissa Pinkola Estés, *Women who Run with the Wolves: Myths and Stories of the Wild Woman Archetype* (New York, 1992), pp. 258–62.

34 Thomson, *People of the Sea*, p. 6. In *Thomas Trew and the Selkie's Curse* (London, 2007) by children's author Sophie Masson, the young Rhymer slips beneath the waves in the company of his selkie companion, to find a great underwater city, where unfortunately for the hungry boy, everything was fishy, seaweedy or odd.

35 Berlie Doherty, *Daughter of the Sea* (London, 1996), p. 115.

36 'The Crofter's Mistake', in Williamson, *Tales of the Seal People*, p. 57.

37 Ibid., p. 59.

38 In March 2012 the Yellowknife Dance Collective performed a tale of Sedna and her husband Raven; www.nnsl.com, accessed 17 March 2014.

39 Sedna is also the name of vodka made in Newfoundland with iceberg water, a product that brings about another kind of transformation in human consumers; www.sednavodka.com, accessed 15 April 2014.

40 Knud Rasmussen, *Eskimo Folk Tales*, ed. and trans. W. Worster (London, 1921); www.gutenberg.org, accessed 19 March 2014. There are many versions of the story of Kiviuk and the seal.

41 Robin Robertson extract from 'Selkie', in *Swithering* (Toronto, 2006). Bear Grylls is the star of a Discovery Channel television series – he dons the seal skin in 'Seal-Skin Wetsuit', uploaded 7 February 2011, www.youtube.com.

42 Thomson, *People of the Sea*, p. xix.

43 Ibid., p. 23.

44 Ibid., p. 7.

4 HUNTING THE SEAL

1 Guillaume de Salluste Du Bartas, cited in Izaak Walton and Charles Cotton, *The Compleat Angler, or Contemplative Man's Recreation, being a Discourse on Rivers, Fish-ponds, Fish, and Fishing* (London, 1835), pp. 58–9.

2 Virgil, *Georgics*, quoted in William M. Johnson and David M. Lavigne, 'Monk Seals in Antiquity: The Mediterranean Monk Seal (*Monachus monachus*)', in *Ancient History and Literature* (Nederlandsche Commissie Voor Internationale Natuurbescherming, Mededelingen No. 35, 1999), p. 17.

3 Aristotle, *Historia Animalium*, Part 6, 12; http://classics.mit.edu, accessed 10 April 2014; Pliny the Elder, 'Vitulina marina', in *Natural History*, ix (15), http://data.perseus.org, accessed 10 April 2014.

4 Plutarch, 'Whether Land or Sea Animals are Cleverer', in *Moralia*, 9, 22; http://penelope.uchicago.edu, accessed 10 April 2014.

5 Galenus, *De alimentorum facultatibus libri iii*, cited in Johnson and Lavigne, 'Monk Seals in Antiquity', p. 36.

6 David Thomson, *The People of the Sea: Celtic Tales of the Seal-folk* (Edinburgh, 1954; 1996; digital edition, 2009), p. 47.

7 Noted in Robert Hamilton, 'The Natural History of the Amphibious Carnivora', in *The Naturalist's Library: Mammalia*, viii (Edinburgh, 1839), p. 136.

8 Briton Cooper Busch, *The War Against the Seals: A History of the North American Seal Fishery* (Montreal, 1985), p. 164.

9 Ken Albala, ed., *Food Cultures of the World Encyclopedia*, vol. i (Santa Barbara, CA, 2011), p. 193.

10 A rise in food poisoning among Alaskan native peoples due to botulism in fermented foods, including seal and seal oil, has been attributed to the introduction of plastic containers. Changes in traditional preparation methods have also been implicated in food poisoning. Recently a family in Greenland died after eating *kiviak*, a special dish of sealskin stuffed with fermented birds. Rather than the traditional auks, eiders were used and being larger, did not ferment completely, resulting in the poisoning.

11 My first feed of flipper pie has always remained with me as a delicacy best helped along with copious amounts of dark rum. More recently Newfoundland chefs have devised new recipes for seal meat, part of a revival of traditional foods.

12 Hamilton, 'Natural History of the Amphibious Carnivora', p. 165. Noted in Thomson, *People of the Sea*, p. 139.

13 Johnson and Lavigne, 'Monk Seals in Antiquity', p. 53. In ski mountaineering in the 1950s, sealskins were fastened to the bottoms of skis to provide grip. Elisabeth Franck, 'Sealskin Skiing', *Departures*, January/February 2011, www.departures.com, accessed 20 March 2014. Contemporary Greenlanders also use this technique; see Ted Kerasote, *Bloodties: Nature, Culture and the Hunt* (New York, 1993), p. 52.

14 William M. Johnson, 'Monk Seals in Post-classical History: The Role of the Mediterranean Monk Seal (*Monachus monachus*)', in *European History and Culture, from the Fall of Rome to the 20th Century* (Nederlandsche Commissie Voor Internationale Natuurbescherming, Mededelingen No. 39, 2004), p. 48.

15 Ibid., pp. 33–7.

16 Johnson and Lavigne, 'Monk Seals in Antiquity', p. 35.

17 Pliny the Elder, *Natural History*, IX (15).

18 Hamilton, 'Natural History of the Amphibious Carnivora', pp. 128–9.

19 Thomson, *People of the Sea*, p. 19.

20 Ibid., p. 185.

21 Pliny the Elder, *Natural History*, XXXII (34), http://data.perseus.org/citations, accessed 20 April 2014.

Hippocrates also recommended an alternative remedy: seal lungs burnt with goat dung and cedar dust. Johnson and Lavigne, 'Monk Seals in Antiquity', p. 77.

22 Johnson and Lavigne, 'Monk Seals in Antiquity', p. 41.

23 Johnson, 'Monk Seals in Post-classical History', pp. 54, 52.

24 Michael Dwyer, from *Over the Side, Mickey*, quoted in Linda Pannozzo, *The Devil and the Deep Blue Sea: An Investigation into the Scapegoating of Canada's Grey Seal* (Halifax, 2013), p. 14.

25 George Anson, *A Voyage Around the World, in the Years MDCXXL, I, II, III, IV*, vol. I (Edinburgh, 1781), pp. 137, 150.

26 'All agree that its quality is most excellent. It is limpid, inodorous, and never becomes rancid; in cooking, it imparts no disagreeable savour; and in burning, it produces no smoke nor smell, and is slow of combustion. In England, it is used for the softening of wool and the manufacture of cloth; and it is also much used in China.' Hamilton, 'Natural History of the Amphibious Carnivora', p. 224.

27 Ibid., pp. 222–3.

28 Busch, *War Against the Seals*, p. 173.

29 Ibid., p. 181.

30 Joseph Banks, quoted in Busch, *War Against the Seals*, p. 29.

31 Elephant seal hunting was finally banned in 1922 by Mexico and in 1923 by the U.S.

32 Joel Asaph Allen, *A History of North American Pinnipeds: A Monograph of the Walruses, Sea-lions, Sea-bears and Seals of North America* (Washington, DC, 1880), pp. 488–9.

33 Quoted in Shannon Ryan, *The Ice Hunters: A History of Newfoundland Sealing to 1914* (St John's, 1994), p. 72.

34 Quoted ibid., p. 106.

35 'Greenspond is a pretty place/ So is Pinchards Island,/ Me Ma will have a new silk dress,/ When me Da comes home from swiling'. Traditional Newfoundland folk song cited in Busch, *War Against the Seals*, p. 58.

36 Beckles Wilson, *The Tenth Island, Being Some Account of Newfoundland, its People, its Politics, its Problems, and its*

Peculiarities (1897; reprint London, 2013), p. 115 (134);
www.forgottenbooks.org, accessed 30 April 2014.

37 Bob Saunders of Greenspond, Bonavista Bay, quoted in J. G. Millais,
   Newfoundland and its Untrodden Ways (London, 1907), p. 42.

38 George Allan England, *Vikings of the Ice: Being the Log of a
   Tenderfoot on the Great Newfoundland Seal Hunt* (Garden City, NJ,
   1924). England wrote in his Prefatory Note: 'For many years the
   Newfoundland seal hunt has been the greatest hunt in the world, and
   that so little has been written about it is a mystery. The world as a
   whole knows little of it.'

39 Ibid., pp. 50, 2. England saw the sealers somewhat differently and
   he dedicated his book to them: 'To the strongest, hardiest, and
   bravest/ men I have ever known/ the sealers of newfoundland/
   this book is/ admiringly dedicated.'

40 Ibid., p. 29. Kean was awarded an Order of the British Empire
   (OBE) when he brought back his one millionth seal pelt.

41 James Murphy, 'Ballad of the Sealers', in St John's *Evening Herald*,
   11 March 1913; quoted in Michael Harrington, *Goin' to the Ice:
   Offbeat History of the Newfoundland Sealfishery* (St John's, 1986), p. vi.

42 Wilson, *The Tenth Island*, p. 114 (133).

43 England, *Vikings*, p. 56. For the modern retelling of this woeful
   tale, see Cassie Brown, *Death on the Ice: The Great Newfoundland
   Sealing Disaster of 1914* (Toronto, 1974). The town of Elliston,
   Newfoundland, is building a memorial to the 1914 sealing disaster, with a sculpture representing this story; www.homefromthe-
   sea.ca, accessed 3 January 2015.

44 From a newspaper article of 1830, quoted in Ryan, *Ice Hunters*,
   p. 101.

45 Crantz, quoted in Hamilton, 'The Natural History of the
   Amphibious Carnivora', pp. 142–3.

46 Cited in A.E.J. Ogilvie et al., 'Seals and Sea Ice in Medieval
   Greenland', *Journal of the North Atlantic* (2009),
   www.nabohome.org, accessed 30 November 2014.

47 Knud Rasmussen, *Across Arctic America: Narrative of the Fifth Thule
   Expedition* (New York, 1927; Fairbanks, AK, 1999), pp. 227–30.

48 Kenojuak, the famed Inuit artist, based one of her earliest prints on the design she had cut for a sealskin bag – 'Rabbit eating Seaweed' (1958).

49 Greenlanders have many names to describe the same animal. The ringed seal is a *neitsek*, called *uuttoq* when sunning on the ice and *puissi* when swimming in a lead. Ted Kerasote, *Bloodties*, p. 16.

50 Hamilton cited Pallas's description of hunting seals by a similar stratagem on the ice of Lake Baikal: 'The hunters . . . put themselves into slight sledges, on which they hoist a white sail. The Seals, taking this for a floating island of ice, are not alarmed, and approach. They are thus surprised and shot, and many are captured.' Hamilton, 'The Natural History of the Amphibious Carnivora', p. 86.

51 Kerasote, *Bloodties*, p. 58.

52 'Jean's Seal Meal Sparks Feeding Frenzy', *Toronto Star*, 27 May 2009, www.thestar.com.

53 *Tungijuq*, www.isuma.tv, accessed 20 April 2014.

5 WHITECOAT

1 Joel Asaph Allen, *A History of North American Pinnnipeds: A Monograph of the Walruses, Sea-lions, Sea-bears and Seals of North America* (Washington, 1880), p. 484.

2 A 'whitecoat' is a harp seal pup less than two weeks old and still bearing lanugo, or fetal fur, normally shed two to three weeks after birth. In the 1950s, Norwegian scientists discovered a way to ensure that the white fur stayed fast to the skins. This increased the value of the pelts as fur.

3 The film is available in two parts on YouTube: *Les Grands Phoques de la banquise*, accessed 2 January 2015; there is also commentary about the film on the archives of Radio-Canada, http://archives.radio-canada.ca, accessed 2 January 2015.

4 Phillip Tocque, quoted in Briton Cooper Busch, *The War Against the Seals: A History of the North American Seal Fishery* (Montreal, 1985), p. 60.

5 Beckles Wilson, *The Tenth Island, Being Some Account of Newfoundland, its People, its Politics, its Problems, and its Peculiarities* (1897; reprint London, 2013), pp. 110 (129), 112 (131); www.forgottenbooks.org, accessed 30 April 2014.

6 Brian Davies, *Red Ice: My Fight to Save the Seals* (nd), p. 15.

7 Ibid., p. 17.

8 George Allan England, *Vikings of the Ice: Being the Log of a Tenderfoot on the Great Newfoundland Seal Hunt* (Garden City, NJ, 1924), p. 164 (p. 98).

9 Paul Watson, *Seal Wars: Twenty-five Years on the Front Lines with Harp Seals* (Toronto, 2002), p. 78.

10 Frank Zelko, *Make It a Green Peace! The Rise of Countercultural Environmentalism* (Oxford, 2013), p. 257.

11 *Sunday Sun*, 5 January 1958, in Robert Lambert, 'The Grey Seal in Britain: A Twentieth-century History of a Nature Conservation Success', *Environment and History*, VIII/4 (November 2002), pp. 449–74 (p. 459); www.jstor.org, accessed 14 May 2014.

12 Davies, *Red Ice*, p. 8.

13 England, *Vikings of the Ice*, p. 90. Seals have from one and a half to two times the volume of blood to body weight greater than other mammals.

14 'It is the slaughter-house, but what pen or abattoir ever had such surroundings as these: the calm silent whiteness of the snow, the stately purity of the icebergs, whose thousand cathedral-like spires and pinnacles glitter in the sun, are little in accord with the bloody nature of this industry.' Wilson, *The Tenth Island*, p. 112.

15 England, *Vikings of the Ice*, p. 107, pp. 86–7.

16 Robert Hamilton, 'The Natural History of the Amphibious Carnivora', in *The Naturalist's Library: Mammalia*, VIII (Edinburgh, 1839), p. 81.

17 Dr Harry Lillie, quoted in Watson, *Seal Wars*, p. 53. The issue of waste in the Newfoundland seal hunt was a matter of concern in the late nineteenth century, with repeated attempts to ban 'panning' of seals (with subsequent loss of pelts to wind

and weather). See Shannon Ryan, *The Ice Hunters: A History of Newfoundland Sealing to 1914* (St John's, 1994), pp. 113–15.

18 Davies, *Red Ice*, pp. 44–5.

19 IFAW, Canada's Commercial Seal Slaughter 2009, p. 6; www.ifaw.org, accessed 15 May 2014.

20 Davies, *Red Ice*, p. 63.

21 Paul Watson called the anti-sealing protests of 1977 'The Labrador Three-ring Circus'.

22 Watson, *Seal Wars*, p. 78.

23 Ibid., pp. 89, 93.

24 Hunter, quoted in Zelko, *Make it a Green Peace!*, p. 267.

25 Brigitte Bardot is an animal rights activist, and in 1986 she founded the Brigitte Bardot Foundation for the Welfare and Protection of Animals. She returned to Canada in 2006 to protest the continuance of the seal hunt.

26 Ray Guy, 'Seal Wars', *Canadian Geographic* (January/February 2000), www.canadiangeographic.ca, accessed 1 May 2014.

27 'Every person who strikes a seal with a club or hakapik shall strike the seal on the top of the cranium until it has been crushed and shall immediately palpate the cranium to confirm that it has been crushed.' Minister of Justice, Marine Mammal Regulations SOR/93–56, May 2014, http://laws-lois.justice.gc.ca, accessed 5 May 2014.

28 Interview with Earle McCurdy, quoted in Willeen Keough, '(Re-) telling Newfoundland Sealing Masculinity: Narrative and Counter-Narrative', *Journal of the Canadian Historical Association*, XXI/1 (2010), pp. 131–50 (p. 141).

29 David F. Pelly, *Sacred Hunt: A Portrait of the Relationship between Seals and Inuit* (Vancouver, 2001), p. 113.

30 Ibid.

31 Cheap souvenir sealskin keychains marked 'Toronto Canada' were sold in the 1960s. At the time of writing high-fashion accessories are created by local artisans in the north as well as in Atlantic Canada. For the new fashion industry, see the work of Ranva Simonsen, an Iqaluit seamstress and business owner who works

with sealskin; 'In Nunavut, sealskin supply can't meet the demand', www.cbc.ca, accessed 1 April 2014; or see the mobile device accessories in sealskin at www.ivalu.ca, accessed 5 January 2015.

32 Aaron Hutchins, 'Canadians Speak Up Against Ellen's Anti-seal Hunt Cause', *Macleans* (25 March 2014), www.macleans.ca, accessed 30 March 2014.

33 Davies, *Red Ice*, p. 46.

34 Keough, '(Re-)telling Newfoundland Sealing Masculinity', p. 139.

35 Busch, *The War Against the Seals*, p. 254.

36 Watson, *Seal Wars*, p. 17.

37 Quoted ibid., p. 129.

38 Ibid., pp. 94–5.

39 Calvin Coish, *Season of the Seal* (St John's, 1979), p. 93.

40 Quoted in Keough, '(Re-)telling Newfoundland Sealing Masculinity', p. 140.

41 Brian Davies and Eliot Porter, *Seal Song* (New York, 1978), p. 89.

42 Quoted in Keough, '(Re-)telling Newfoundland Sealing Masculinity', pp. 139–40.

43 Ibid., p. 138.

44 Quoted in Cynthia Lamson, '*Bloody Decks and a Bumper Crop*': *The Rhetoric of Sealing Counter-protest* (St John's, 1979), p. 14.

45 Ibid., p. 18.

46 Quoted ibid., p. 80.

47 Keough, '(Re-)telling Newfoundland Sealing Masculinity', p. 144.

48 Davies, *Red Ice*, p. 35.

49 Quoted in IFAW (2009), p. 30.

50 It is, however, legal to kill very young seal pups that have lost their white coat, what the sealers call 'raggedy jackets'.

51 'Brigitte Bardot's Crusade to Save Canada's Seals', *The Independent*, 24 March 2006, www.independent.co.uk.

52 Quoted in 'East Coast Seal Hunt Starts amid ongoing Court Case, Trade Challenge', *Globe and Mail*, 14 April 2014.

53 On 10 October 2014, the EU and Canada agreed to the unhindered import and sale of sealskins from Nunavut's Inuit hunters; see 'Europe Allows Inuit Sealskins', 20 October 2014, www.nnsl.com.

54 In response the Humane Society initiated the 'Chefs for Seals' campaign, www.humanesociety.org, accessed 3 January 2015.

55 And continue today. A headline in the newspaper *The Mirror* on 26 November 2014 screamed: 'Killer Grey Seals could be on the Loose in British Waters, a New Report Warns', www.mirror.co.uk/news.

56 Linda Pannozzo, *The Devil and the Deep Blue Sea: An Investigation into the Scapegoting of Canada's Grey Seal* (Halifax, 2013), p. 1.

57 Even IKEA has joined in. I purchased a plush mother seal with whitecoat 'pup' attached in the nursery section in 2013.

58 Quoted in Jeremy Cherfas, 'Rationality and the Slaughter of Seals', *New Scientist*, LXVII/1094 (March 1978), pp. 724–6 (p. 726).

59 And can offer comfort in return: 'A Japanese robot resembling a baby seal, which responds amiably to stroking and can distinguish voices, seems to help elderly patients with dementia'. Noted in 'Rise of the Robots', *The Economist*, 29 March 2014, p. 13.

60 Brigitte Bardot, 'Brigitte Bardot Carries Her Crusade for the Baby Seals to Newfoundland's Icy Battleground', *People*, VII/14 (April 1977), www.people.com, accessed 30 April 2014.

61 Davies and Porter, *Seal Song*, p. 12.

62 England, *Vikings of the Ice*, p. 83.

63 Quoted in Davies and Porter, *Seal Song*, p. 90.

64 Ibid., p. 13.

Select Bibliography

Allen, Joel Asaph, *A History of North American Pinnipeds: A Monograph of the Walruses, Sea-lions, Sea-bears and Seals of North America* (Washington, DC, 1880)

Brown, Cassie, *Death on the Ice: The Great Newfoundland Sealing Disaster of 1914* (Toronto, 1974)

Bruemmer, Fred, *The Life of the Harp Seal* (Montreal, 1977)

Busch, Briton Cooper, *The War Against the Seals: A History of the North American Seal Fishery* (Montreal, 1985)

Carroll, Michael, *The Seal and Herring Fisheries of Newfoundland: Together with a Condensed History of the Island* (Montreal, 1873)

Coish, Calvin, *Season of the Seal* (St John's, 1979)

Cooper, Susan, *The Selkie Girl* (New York, 1986)

Davies, Brian, *Red Ice: My Fight to Save the Seals* (nd)

—, and Eliot Porter, *Seal Song* (New York, 1978)

Doherty, Berlie, *Daughter of the Sea* (London, 1996)

England, George Allan, *Vikings of the Ice: Being the Log of a Tenderfoot on the Great Newfoundland Seal Hunt* (Garden City, NJ, 1924)

Farre, Rowena, *Seal Morning* [1957] (Leicester, 1975)

Goodridge, Harry and Lew Dietz, *A Seal Called Andre: The Two Worlds of a Maine Harbour Seal* (New York, 1975)

Hamilton, Robert, 'The Natural History of the Amphibious Carnivora', in *The Naturalist's Library: Mammalia*, VIII (Edinburgh, 1839)

Harrington, Michael, *Goin' to the Ice: Offbeat History of the Newfoundland Sealfishery* (St John's, 1986)

Jackson, Melanie, *The Selkie Bride* (New York, 2010)

Johnson, William M., 'Monk Seals in Post-classical History: The Role of the Mediterranean Monk Seal (*Monachus monachus*)', in *European History and Culture, from the Fall of Rome to the 20th Century* (Nederlandsche Commissie Voor Internationale Natuurbescherming, Mededelingen No. 39, 2004)

—, and David M. Lavigne, 'Monk Seals in Antiquity: The Mediterranean Monk Seal (*Monachus monachus*)', in *Ancient History and Literature* (Nederlandsche Commissie Voor Internationale Natuurbescherming, Mededelingen No. 35, 1999)

Jones, Ken, *Seal Doctor: The Delightful Story of Ken Jones and his Orphan Seals* (Glasgow, 1978)

Kerasote, Ted, *Bloodties: Nature, Culture and the Hunt* (New York, 1993)

King, Judith, *Seals of the World* (London, 1964)

Lamson, Cynthia, *'Bloody Decks and a Bumper Crop': The Rhetoric of Sealing Counter-protest* (St John's, 1979)

Lockley, R. M., *The Saga of the Grey Seal: Introducing the Natural History of the Grey Seal of the North Atlantic* (New York, 1955)

—, *Seal-woman* (New York, 1975)

Pannozzo, Linda, *The Devil and the Deep Blue Sea: An Investigation into the Scapegoating of Canada's Grey Seal* (Halifax, 2013)

Pelly, David F., *Sacred Hunt: A Portrait of the Relationship Between Seals and Inuit* (Vancouver, 2001)

Rasmussen, Knud, *Across Arctic America: Narrative of the Fifth Thule Expedition* (New York, 1927; Fairbanks, AK, 1999)

Riedman, Marianne, *The Pinnipeds: Seals, Sea Lions and Walruses* (Berkeley, CA, 1990)

Ryan, Shannon, *The Ice Hunters: A History of Newfoundland Sealing to 1914* (St John's, 1994)

Rybczynski, Natalia, Mary R. Dawson and Richard H. Tedford, 'A Semi-aquatic Arctic Mammalian Carnivore from the Miocene Epoch and Origin of Pinnipedia', *Nature*, CDLVIII/23 (April 2009), pp. 1021–4

Scheffer, Victor B., *Seals, Sea Lions and Walruses: A Review of the Pinnipedia* (Stanford, CA, 1958)

Thomson, David, *The People of the Sea: Celtic Tales of the Seal-folk* [1954] (Edinburgh, 1996; digital edition, 2009)

Watson, Paul, *Seal Wars: Twenty-five Years on the Front Lines with Harp Seals* (Toronto, 2002)

Williams, Terrie, *The Odyssey of KP2: An Orphan Seal, A Marine Biologist and the Fight to Save a Species* (New York, 2012)

Williamson, Duncan, *Tales of the Seal People: Scottish Folk Tales* (Northampton, MA, 2000)

Associations and Websites

ASSOCIATIONS

Association des chasseurs de phoques des Îles-de-la-Madeleine (in French and English)
The Magdalen Islands sealhunters' website in defence of the hunt
www.chasseursdephoques.com

Canadian Sealers Association
www.sealharvest.ca

Harpseals.org
www.harpseals.org

The Humane Society of the United States
www.humanesociety.org/issucs/seal_hunt

International Fund for Animal Welfare
www.ifaw.org/canada/our-work/saving-seals

Inuit Sila (in Danish and English)
Supporters of the Inuit hunt in Greenland
http://inuitsila.org

PETA: Canadian Seal Slaughter
www.peta.org/issues/animals-used-for-clothing/fur/
canadian-seal-slaughter

Seal Conservation Society
www.pinnipeds.org

Sea Shepherd
www.seashepherd.org/seals

Seals and Sealing Network
www.sealsandsealing.net

WEBSITES

Canadian Museum of Nature, 'Puijila, A Prehistoric Walking Seal'
http://nature.ca/puijila

EarthGuide, Elephant Seals
http://earthguide.ucsd.edu/elephantseals

Fisheries and Oceans Canada: Seals and Sealing
www.dfo-mpo.gc.ca/fm-gp/seal-phoque

Government of Nunavut: Sustainable Sealing in a Traditional
Economy
www.sealingnunavut.ca

Home from the Sea: Sealers Memorial
www.homefromthesea.ca

Icelandic Seal Centre
www.selasetur.is

IUCN Red List of Threatened Species
www.iucnredlist.org

Monachus-guardian.org
www.monachus-guardian.org

National Film Board of Canada, Netsilik Eskimo
www.nfb.ca/subjects/inuit/netsilik

National Oceanic and Atmospheric Administration (NOAA),
Northeast Fisheries Science Center, Seal Research
www.nefsc.noaa.gov/psb/seals

National Oceanic and Atmospheric Administration (NOAA), Pacific
Islands Fisheries Science Center, Hawaiian Monk Seal Research
Program (HMSRP)
www.pifsc.noaa.gov/hawaiian_monk_seal

North Atlantic Seal Research Consortium (NASRC)
http://nasrc.whoi.edu

Seal Sanctuary
www.sealsanctuary.co.uk

Seals, Naturally Scottish
www.snh.org.uk/publications/on-line/naturallyscottish/seals/law.asp

Tungijuq (What We Eat)
Inuit jazz throat-singer Tanya Tagaq and Cannes-winning film-maker
Zacharias Kunuk
www.isuma.tv

Weddell Seal Science
http://weddellsealscience.com

Acknowledgements

I owe a great debt of gratitude to all those who have lived beside, studied and in some cases, loved the seals. I also want to thank those scientists, naturalists and photographers who have so generously made their observations and images available on the Internet to enable everyone to share their knowledge of the people of the sea.

I also want to express my thanks to Jonathan Burt, for his vision in conceiving the Animal series and supporting its authors as they seek to understand the histories of the others with whom we inhabit the terraqueous globe. My thanks as well to the publisher and staff at Reaktion Books for their thoughtful advice and courteous assistance. Finally, my thanks to my husband and children, who with me have followed the trails that lead to the secret places of the seals.

Photo Acknowledgements

The author and publishers wish to express their thanks to the below sources of illustrative material and / or permission to reproduce it.

Courtesy of the author: p. 10; © Robert Bailey, www.robertbailey-photography.com: p. 71; The British Museum, London, photos © Trustees of the British Museum: pp. 82, 88, 90, 105, 107, 119, 134 (top), 135, 137 (top), 138, 141; iStock.com/floridastock: p. 170; iStock.com/michaklootwijk: p. 6; James Vey Collection, St John's, Newfoundland: p. 125; Library of Congress, Prints and Photographs Division, Washington, DC: pp. 21, 137 (bottom); photo Patrick Moore, courtesy of Patrick Moore: p. 153; Museum of Archaeology and Anthropology, Cambridge: p. 102; NOAA Central Library, National Oceanic and Atmospheric Administration, Silver Spring, Maryland: pp. 24, 25 (top), 38 (top), 46, 56, 92, 120; NOAA Central Library, National Oceanic and Atmospheric Administration, photo Ray Boland, NOAA/NMFS/PIFD/ESOD: p. 79, photo Michael Cameron, NOAA/NMFS/AKFCS/NMM: p. 39, photo Captain Budd Christman, NOAA Corps: pp. 24, 25, photo Dr Mike Goebel, NOAA NMFS SWFSC, Antarctic Marine Living Resources (AMLR) Program: p. 91, photo Dr James P. McVey, NOAA Sea Grant Program: p. 29, photo Barbara Taylor NMFS /SWFSC/PRD, NOAA Fisheries: p. 33; photo Beau Richter (this photograph was taken under the authority of NMFS permit number 13602–1): p. 78; courtesy of Christine Sheppard: p. 47; photo Sipa Press/REX Shutterstock: p. 156; courtesy of the artist (Nobumichi Tamura): p. 15; Victoria & Albert Museum, London: pp. 41, 89, 98, 113, 127; photo Stan Waterman,

Index